The Author

Gary Wood (Bsc[Hons], PgC, PhD, FHEA, CSci, CPsycho ... FbPsS) is a social psychologist, personal development coach and broadcaster. He combines a solid academic background with an engaging style and works with companies and individuals to translate evidence-based psychology and coaching into down-to-earth, workable solutions. He has taught psychology and learning skills in several UK universities and regularly appears on radio and television offering expert analysis and coaching tips. He has been an agony uncle for magazines and websites and is widely quoted in the press. Gary is a Chartered Psychologist, a Fellow of the Higher Education Academy, a Chartered Scientist and a Chartered Member of The British Psychological Society's Special Group for Coaching Psychology. He runs his own coaching and training practice and research consultancy in Birmingham and Edinburgh. In his spare time he eats, sleeps, reads and occasionally sings. *Unlock Your Confidence* is his third book and is based on his confidence-building workshops.

Also by Dr. Gary Wood

Sex, Lies and Stereotypes: Challenging Views of Women, Men and Relationships
Don't Wait For Your Ship to Come In . . . Swim Out To Meet It!

UNLOCK YOUR CONFIDENCE

FIND THE KEYS
TO LASTING CHANGE
THROUGH THE
CONFIDENCE-KARMA METHOD

DR. GARY WOOD

WATKINS PUBLISHING
LONDON

This edition published in the UK and USA in 2013 by
Watkins Publishing Limited, Sixth Floor,
75 Wells Street, London W1T 3QH

A member of Osprey Group

1 3 5 7 9 10 8 6 4 2

Designed and typeset by Donald Sommerville

Printed and bound in Italy by L.E.G.O. S.p.A.

A CIP record for this book is available from the British Library

ISBN: 978-1-78028-595-5

www.watkinspublishing.co.uk

Distributed in the USA and Canada by Sterling Publishing Co., Inc.
387 Park Avenue South, New York, NY 10016-8810

Contents

Acknowledgements

I'd like at acknowledge the help and support I received along the way in writing this book.

First and foremost thanks to Sandra Rigby at Watkins Publishers for getting behind this project from the start and her help in honing and refining the manuscript. Thanks also to all the team at Watkins for support and guidance throughout the process, and Donald Sommerville for his eye for detail and valuable suggestions during typesetting. Stand-up comic Billy Rubin also helped with a few choice turns of phrase. I also wish to thank The Society of Authors for contractual advice and The Authors' Foundation (Society of Authors) for a grant to support the completion of the book. Thanks also to Jo Hemmings for advice in the early stages of this project. Thank you to my parents Shirley and Bill Wood for the loan of their computer when mine gave up the ghost a week before the deadline and also Access Computers who managed to save the contents of my hard drive. I gained valuable insights from working with people attending my confidence-building workshops which helped me to put some important final touches to the book. Thanks also to my coaching clients who never cease to inspire me too. It's always good to be reminded that learning (like confidence) is a two-way street. Last but not least, special thanks to Takeshi Fujisawa for ceaseless help, encouragement, software support and cake.

Gary Wood

This book is dedicated to my Nan, Nelly Florence Butcher (née Balnaves) for her sense of humour and unconditional positive regard and to my grand-niece, Isla Seren Young for the sense of optimism and joy she brings and the opportunity to play again.

It is also dedicated to courage.

The Intro

Life is not easy for any of us. But what of that? We must
have perseverance and above all confidence in ourselves. We
must believe that we are gifted for something and that this
thing must be attained.

Marie Curie, 1867–1934, physicist and chemist

Confidence: Gift or Process?

True confidence embraces and harnesses your capabilities enabling
you to seize new opportunities and take on new challenges with
hope and with trust in yourself. So, if you've ever missed a chance
in life because you let your inner voice of self-doubt talk you out
of it, then the *Confidence-Karma Approach* is for you.

Have you ever wanted to take the driving seat in your life
instead of settling for the back seat? Have you ever shunned
an opportunity and said 'no' when you longed to say 'yes'?
Living with confidence is about living with courage rather than
habitually cowering in fear. So if it's time for you to make better
choices and seize life's chances, or even if you just want to feel
more comfortable in your own skin, then read on.

It's tempting to see confidence as an elusive gift bestowed
on the chosen few. Nothing could be further from the truth.
Confidence is not an all-or-nothing gift, it's an on-going process.
When we talk about 'losing confidence', it is really just an
interruption in that process. We all have the inherent abilities for
confidence building. It's your birthright. To regain this birthright

(and unlock your confidence) you do not need to walk on hot coals, break wooden planks with your hands or throw yourself out of aeroplanes. In fact many people would prefer to do any of these rather than tackle public speaking, ask someone out on a date, or get involved in other aspects of everyday life or special occasions.

Confidence is not a scarce commodity. There's plenty to go around. True confidence rubs off on to others. In fact, it's positively infectious. What you need is everyday inner confidence not confidence tricks. Confidence is gained and regained in the same way you learned everything else from the day you were born, that is, in meaningful, purposeful, baby steps and with a little courage and persistence. Many people just want to be able to walk into a room full of strangers and chill out, not freak out!

Unlock Your Confidence offers a complete personal-development programme to attain true inner confidence based on the *Confidence-Karma Approach*. It draws on evidence-based psychology, learning theory, teaching practice, elements of psychotherapy, and insights from professional experience in coaching and training. It reveals the keys to confidence through explanations, exercises, anecdotes, diagrams and opportunities to carry out personal experiments This book won't give you all the answers. It gives you something far more precious. It shows you how to ask better questions. Once you begin to ask the right questions and start providing your own answers you are more likely to own and act on self-realizations, and you are more likely to pass on your own eureka moments to others. Many of the tools and techniques will help you to question the relationship between the self and others and its implications in confidence-building. That's a fundamental principle in the *Confidence-Karma Approach*.

Self and Others

Some people get to grips with the confidence-building process more quickly than others. I declare that I was a confidence 'late bloomer'. Two situations changed my outlook. First, I went island-hopping alone in Greece. Second, I began teaching psychology.

All About Me

When I went on holiday alone for the first time I realized I had to take responsibility for all aspects of my experience. This included sitting alone in a café in a picturesque harbour without feeling that I had to pretend to be reading a book. I didn't have to signal to others that I had a purpose in being alone. I could just sit there enjoying the present moment. It was genuinely the first time in my life that I had felt truly comfortable in my own skin. It wasn't about other people, it was all about me.

All About Others

By contrast, standing up in front of a group of part-time mature students ceased to be just about me. It was all about them. They had an abundance of motivation and certainly showed courage in taking the plunge to take a new direction in life. However, many of them lacked confidence.

So to build on my training in psychology and teaching I took an intensive coaching-skills course (the first of many). Armed with new insights and skills I developed several extracurricular personal development courses for my students. These formed the basis for my book *Don't Wait for Your Ship to Come In . . . Swim Out to Meet It*. Although my initial goal was to help others, I achieved a personal goal in the process. This also opened up another opportunity for me and I began providing one-to-one coaching. This has become one of the most rewarding aspects of my work.

Since my career now involves 'talking for a living', it's rather a turnaround from school when I dreaded speaking in public. My biggest fear at school was reading aloud in class. I'd hesitate and stutter over the words, much to the amusement of my classmates. Reading alone was never a problem, only when I had an audience.

Throughout this book I include case studies as well as snippets from my own journey. The case studies are composites, with details altered to protect anonymity. All people alluded to also gave permission for me to discuss general scenarios. The case studies and personal anecdotes highlight how I made the connections that developed my coaching practice and led to this book. *Unlock Your Confidence* didn't take nearly as long to write as it has to live it. This book offers you a short cut, so you can get on with living with confidence right now.

What Goes Around Comes Around

The most satisfying aspect of my work is getting the opportunity to make a difference in the lives of others. Mostly this is helping people learn how to learn. There have been a number of guiding lights in my life and one of my core values is to pass this on. So the *Confidence-Karma Approach* has been developed to help anyone discover the master keys to unlocking confidence in themselves and in others. It looks inwards and outwards and so avoids the 'me me me' trap. Taking care of oneself is a good thing but not to the exclusion of all else. We are social beings and confidence is framed by our interactions in the social world. It's rather difficult to be confident or shy on a desert island with no one to share your coconuts!

The concept of karma is found in many cultures and is popularly defined as the principle that 'what goes around, comes around' in that we reap what we sow in life. However, karma is also a pertinent concept for personal development and in particular confidence building. Karma means 'action'. Writer, artist and politician, Johann Wolfgang von Goethe (1749–1832) said 'Knowing is not enough; we must apply, willing is not enough; we must do.' This is in stark contrast to a line from an online review of my previous book. Initially I was perplexed but now it just makes me smile. It read:

> 'This book is an average self-help book, as you do need to apply the advice within if you are to gain something.'

The implication is that a really good self-help book is one that magically transforms you just by you reading it or stroking the cover. However, that attitude leads to more 'shelf-development' than 'self-development'. The books may look lovely on your bookcase but aren't really doing much except collecting dust. *Unlock Your Confidence* is all about an equitable return on your investment. If you invest your money and buy the book, you get a book. If you invest your time and read the book, you get the insight. If you take action and invest time and energy in putting the insights into practice you will get results. The magic comes from doing. Wishful thinking is just the beginning, not an end in itself. The film *The Wizard of Oz* provides us with an eternal truth. None of the main characters would have gained courage, compassion and the ability to learn just by reading the Oz holiday brochure. It was all about the journey. Ultimately the choice is yours. Do you want a book, insight or results? If you commit to the process you can have all three! Why short-change yourself?

Eureka Moments

We all get flashes of inspiration from time to time. Sometimes our brains make connections when we least expect it. I had three such eureka moments that inspired the *Confidence-Karma Approach*, and they also gave me the idea for a simple concept that seemed to summarize neatly a number of key principles in psychology. These insights also helped me to tap into my own skills, strengths and experience to inspire this new twist on confidence coaching that helps my clients get the results they desire.

Insight One

Reviewing my notes after a particularly intense coaching session with a client, let's call her Jenny, I saw that I had scribbled 'like prejudice' in the margin. It occurred to me that the client's perceived lack of confidence was grounded in the relentlessly negative attitudes towards herself that prevented her from taking action on her goals. The origin of attitude in Latin is 'fit and ready for action' and Jenny clearly was not, despite having the skills. It was then that I began to formulate the idea of **auto-prejudice** and the way we can block our own confidence rather than build it. I'll say more about this concept later.

Insight Two

Around the same time as the auto-prejudice insight, I was running team-building workshops for a university's management development programme. My sessions were meant to be fun and experiential rather than 'chalk and talk'. However, one manager (whom we'll call John) took great exception to the ice-breaking warm-up exercise. It was only a game to help people remember each other's names. It never occurred to me that it would provoke such an extreme reaction. John said he didn't want to take part and I just tried to reassure him that it was only a bit of fun to get us in the mood. John stood up, thrust his hand forward in a halt gesture and bellowed quite theatrically and aggressively 'NO! I DO NOT WISH TO TAKE PART.' I suspect that John's work supervisor had 'diagnosed' John's problem as a lack of assertiveness and probably sent him on a course to remedy it. The result was that John just had better skills to argue for his limitations and defences. What John needed was something to challenge his auto-prejudice that things are set up to make him look foolish. To counter this, perhaps a few sessions of coaching might have been more appropriate, tailor-made to John's needs. It was probably a boost in **self-esteem** rather than assertiveness that he needed. It's an often overlooked factor in confidence building.

Insight Three

The next day I visited a friend whose son was a habitual TV channel surfer. As he made a whistle-stop tour of every channel in a matter of minutes, a segment of a programme on bridge building jumped out at me: **the triangle is the most stable and strongest of shapes.** The three points of the triangle in turn made me think of the special significance that the number three has in psychology. Many models and theories use key principles or concepts, such as Sigmund Freud's Id, Ego and Superego and Eric Berne's Parent, Adult and Child. In my area of psychology, attitude formation, there is a similar idea of working through our feelings, actions and thoughts (more on this in the next section). So this led me to consider the triangle as a simple device to represent psychological principles pictorially. For confidence building, this helps us to cut straight to the heart of a theory without getting bogged down in detail. In Chapter 6 we'll consider a number of psychological theories in this way, in order to create a shift in perspective and see ourselves and the confidence-building process from different angles.

Here's how I put the three eureka insights together.

Fit and Ready for Action – Confidence-Karma Triangles

Unlock Your Confidence employs a number of insights from social psychology, recognizing that self-image is a product of us being social animals. It also draws direct parallels between attitude formation and confidence building. Attitudes are general feelings, thoughts and evaluations, including our beliefs, which create 'a mental state of readiness' to respond behaviourally. Similarly, confidence is an assessment of our ability to effect change. First we assess whether there is a way to make a change and then whether or not we are up to it. In the team-building session with John he pre-judged the intention and assumed that the purpose of the exercise was to make him look silly. On the second day of the course, once he had seen that everyone was having fun, he chose to join in. He also said 'It's a good job you've changed things today as yesterday was bloody awful.' Actually, I hadn't changed anything. His attitude had changed and so did his readiness to take part.

Attitudes and confidence are both formed from feelings, thoughts and actions. This led to the first Confidence-Karma triangle – The Big FAT Confidence Triangle.

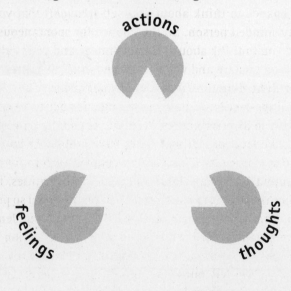

The Big FAT Confidence Triangle

These three components are interrelated. As we learn and make sense of the world we can begin from any angle. Sometimes an action stirs feelings that we later make sense of. At other times we may have a feeling, rationalize and take action. In *Unlock Your Confidence*, we approach confidence building from all three angles.

When approaching an exercise in the book, you may feel slightly uncomfortable or silly. So do you let this override the thought and prevent you from taking action or take action in spite of the feeling? If you do give it a go, then you'll have new information to think about. This will impact on your feelings and the likelihood of taking action the next time. In everyday life you may get an opportunity to act spontaneously, such as helping someone off the bus with a pushchair or reaching something from a supermarket shelf to help an older customer (*action*). This may make you feel good (*feeling*) and so you may be more likely to do it again. It also gives you chance to think about yourself (*thought*) that you are a community-minded person. So the chance for spontaneous action has caused you to think about your self-image and your values, the type of person you are and what you stand for. This is pretty much what you will be doing in *Unlock Your Confidence*.

The Feelings–Actions–Thoughts triangle is applied in the realm of prejudice and discrimination. Prejudice is usually irrational and operates at the level of feelings. Laws have prohibited hate speech such as racist comments. This is often coupled with rational arguments surrounding human rights and equal opportunities. The idea is that people then come to reappraise their feelings and so prejudice is reduced. That's the general idea. As I was coaching Jenny, the links between confidence building and prejudice reduction became more apparent. Auto-prejudice is like an autobiography. It's the on-going story we tell ourselves based on our perceptions (our feelings) of the way others behave towards us and the things they say. We add to this our own thoughts as we try to rationalize. We look for evidence to support the feelings, which in turn informs our actions. On paper Jenny had the qualifications to apply for jobs but let her feelings get in the way. The easiest way to prevent unpleasant feelings is to refrain from doing activities that cause them, even if those actions are in our best interest.

Our self-evaluation is called self-esteem, our sense of self-worth. Implicit within this are the questions 'Am I worth it?' and 'Is it worth it?' In confidence building, self-esteem acts as the stabilizing factor, the bridge between 'faking it' and 'making it', that is from outer display of confidence to true, inner confidence. This leads to the second confidence triangle. So confidence comprises our **self-image**, **self-efficacy**, which is how we judge our abilities to operate in the world, and **self-esteem**, which underpins everything.

The Complete Inner Confidence Triangle

People with low self-worth (esteem) are not truly confident even though they may put on a convincing display. You can't brag, boast, preen, peacock-strut, belittle, bully or bitch your way to confidence, although some people will insist on trying. Confidence is not about making ourselves feel better at the expense of others. If what you're passing on belittles others then it ain't confidence! Some people just like to hear the sound of their own voices, as it drowns out the screams of self-doubt. It's all bluff and bluster.

Some confidence approaches are all about 'outer' manifestations of confidence. You may be cajoled into walking on hot coals or bungee jumping, reasoning that if you can do these dangerous activities you can do anything. The huge assumption is that dare-devil activities and thrill-seeking are part of what we truly value in life, the things we stand for. In fact people may not necessarily make the internal connections (between actions, feelings and thoughts) and translate this sort of activity into everyday empowerment. It could be that some people are so desperate that they don't care about their personal safety. If you don't value yourself then you can take risks as you have nothing to lose. That's not true, inner confidence. If we don't address esteem issues and personal values then all we really have is a recipe for risk-taking. True confidence is definitely about bravery and courage but not about recklessness. Sometimes you can 'fake it 'til you make it', but what's better than starting with the genuine article? By putting self-esteem back into the equation and by exploring attitudes and auto-prejudice we have a powerful model for change that can be used as a framework for your own exploration after you have finished reading this book.

Too Much of a Good Thing?

There is no such thing as 'too much confidence'. If it seems that way, then it's not the genuine article. It's still 'faking it'. What we call 'over-confidence' is not confidence at all. It's a smoke screen for low self-esteem. In *Unlock Your Confidence* the ultimate goal is quiet, inner confidence. Being comfortable in your own skin begins with the ability to relax. That's the basis from which all else proceeds. Relaxation is also the best state in which we learn and so is the best place to be when we try to make changes. Since we all have the ability to relax this puts confidence within the reach of everyone. Confident people aren't the ones who walk into a room and put on a display and make others feel uncomfortable. True confidence puts others at ease. Confident people bring out the best in the people around them. So focus on taking control of your ability to relax, build on your strengths, live according to your values, set goals and seize opportunities to pass on confidence to others. Confidence is a process and always a work in progress.

Unlock Your Confidence contains a chapter on each aspect of the confidence-building process and how they all link together.

How to Get the Most from This Book

I've arranged the material in this book based on core teaching and learning principles. The layout of this book mimics the way we learn most effectively. Once you've finished this introduction, flick through the book to get a feel for the layout. Context helps us to process information more effectively, so each chapter begins with a quotation and a summary to set the scene. The exercises in the main body of the chapter help you to link the material to your own experience. The reminders and prompts for reflection (thoughts and feelings) at the end of the chapters help to consolidate what you have learned. Each chapter concludes with a review of the model that underpins the book plus a **Karma Call**, a guide to things you can start doing right away, however small, that will start making a difference. To get the most out of the book, I recommend that you work through the exercises from cover to cover rather than cherry pick. It will help to keep a personal development journal or have a notebook to hand. Writing things down means that we use more cognitive processes. It slows down our thinking and means we are less likely to jump to conclusions. Taking the time to work through the exercises thoroughly will help to integrate the triple aspects of feelings, actions and thoughts and help you discover the keys to lasting change.

Confidence Triangles

The confidence-triangle learning devices throughout the book offer a shorthand way of remembering key points and concepts. Copy them into a notebook and carry them with you and reflect on them throughout your day. Take any opportunity to explain the principle to other people. In Chapter 3, I offer a short confidence-triangle meditation exercise.

Tools for Change

The *Confidence-Karma Approach* uses three main tools for change that I also use in my coaching practice and have found to be very effective. The questioning techniques are gentle but persistent. The questions focus on your own strengths and ability to find solutions, and encourage small changes in your attitudes and behaviour. At first the questions may seem a little odd, almost clumsy. This is intentional. But please trust in the process and take time to answer all of the questions, using your journal or notebook, even though the questions are sometimes only subtly different. It is through this repetition that this style of thinking becomes second nature. You can also use this style of questioning to help build confidence in others.

The other technique is the scaling question. Sometimes when it's difficult to sum up how you think or feel in words, a simple score out of ten allows you to quantify your attitude so that you can begin to look for solutions more quickly. Scaling questions also offer a simple and effective way to monitor progress.

The third tool is the use of personal experiments. These are invitations to try things out without the threat of failure, since all we are interested in is the feedback from the results, irrespective of what the result actually was. Also take time to keep a record of your personal experiences in your journal or notebook.

All of these techniques are from Solution Focus Brief Therapy and Motivational Interviewing and are incredibly powerful and require you to take an active part in your personal development.

What's Next? – Step-By-Step

The *Confidence-Karma* process begins by establishing what's going on for you right now. It's about getting an idea of what confidence means for you. It's very much how I would work with you as a client in the coaching process.

Chapter 1 offers self-evaluation exercises in confidence and esteem and also looks at your definition of confidence and the attitudes it entails. The chapter also offers a model explaining how all the various aspects of confidence building fit together and how various components in the model control and influence each other. Subsequent chapters explore each component of the model, with various exercises so that you experience and understand how the model works.

Chapter 2 continues the self-evaluation process by considering how confidence fluctuates in different environments and the factors that may affect it. It also gets you to consider your skills and strengths. The *Confidence-Karma Approach* is always about building on what you already have.

Chapter 3 explores the mind–body connection, in particular relaxation, the cornerstone of confidence building. The various exercises are to help you control stress, get in touch with your body and consider the impact of health on confidence.

Building on the mind–body insights, **Chapter 4** offers tips and exercises for creating positive first impressions, improving communication skills, including use of body language, and developing assertiveness. This chapter is useful for developing confidence in others too.

Chapter 5 is the heart of *Unlock Your Confidence* and the *Confidence-Karma Approach*. It deals with values and attitudes. These are the real drivers and shapers of our behaviour and our lives, and the fundamental keys to unlocking your confidence

Chapter 6 introduces a number of psychological principles and how these impact on confidence building, using the triangle device. The aim of this chapter is to get you to consider your feelings, actions and thoughts from different perspectives.

Chapter 7 addresses resistance to change and suggests tools for building resilience and coping.

Chapter 8 begins the process of raising aspirations by exploring how our inner dialogue and imagination impact on confidence building.

Chapter 9 continues the process of raising aspirations by considering goals and the benefit of linking them with values and strengths.

The whole process is rounded off in **Chapter 10** with special exercises to help you consolidate your learning experiences using the *Confidence-Karma Approach*.

So take a deep breath and let the journey to a more confident you begin.

Gary Wood
(info@drgarywood.co.uk)

Chapter 1

Here and Now:
Getting an Angle on It

The real voyage of discovery consists not in seeking new landscapes but in having new eyes.

Marcel Proust, 1871–1922, novelist, critic and essayist

Preview

To begin the whole confidence-building process this chapter provides self-evaluation quizzes in self-confidence and self-esteem. The results of these are used to get an idea of your starting point, a baseline by which you can assess the changes. It also looks at definitions of confidence and esteem and a model (the *Confidence-Karma Chain*) to show how all aspects of the process fit together. Also, by exploring your personal definition of confidence, it provides you with the raw material for your development goals.

Here and Now

A tourist stopped a local person to ask for directions to a famous landmark and the local answered, 'Well I wouldn't start from here!'

In reality 'here and now' are the most important things we have. A main theme of *Confidence Karma* is: **always to build on what you have rather than to obsess over what you don't have.** Situations and conditions could always be better. Many decisions in life are made with incomplete information. Think of your journey to greater confidence as being like a move to a new home. This chapter gives the home setting on your SatNav – where you are right now. Then the following chapters will help you reach your new destination of improved confidence. So throughout this chapter keeping asking yourself, 'What would greater confidence actually mean to me? And, when I have it, what will I be doing then that I'm not doing now?' This will form the basis of concrete goals to work towards.

Big FAT Confidence Definition

When we start to consider the meaning of the word 'confidence', recurring themes emerge including **faith, assurance** and **trust** – here is another FAT triangle. We talk about 'taking someone into our confidence', so confidence clearly also involves relationships with other people we may confide in and trust with our secrets. Confidence is also the state of being certain. When we speak of **self-confidence** we are speaking of our faith and certainty in our ability to operate in the world, to predict that a course of action is correct and most effective. It is also our ability to take that action and to effect the changes we desire so that we continue to grow and develop. And finally, confidence is also about being bold and showing courage.

How Confident Are You?

Let's begin the process with a simple rating using a scale from 0 to 10 to rate your overall confidence level: 0 means 'no confidence at all' and equates to someone unconscious or in a coma; 1 equates to 'just about enough confidence to function at a minimal level'; 5 means 'average confidence'; 8 or 9 mean 'very high confidence' and 10 means 'supreme confidence'. Use any point on the scale that best reflects your attitude.

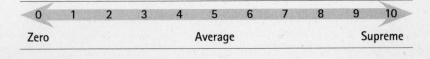

0	1	2	3	4	5	6	7	8	9	10
Zero					Average					Supreme

Get out your journal or notebook and consider the questions below which begin the on-going process of shining a light on your existing strengths and looking at how you might build on them to reach higher levels of confidence.

- How have you got this far along the scale? How did you do this?
- What is it that has helped you to get from 0 to where you are now?
- What can you imagine doing if you move one point up the scale?

By answering these questions you can see that you've already acquired some skill in building confidence.

Now let's explore the issues relating to self-confidence in more detail by answering the following confidence quiz.

Confidence Quiz

The quiz comprises 20 questions. Indicate your level of agreement with each item, without 'over-thinking'. There will be plenty of time to reflect later. The quiz is in two parts and the scoring reverses for the second part. For the first part, score each of the statements on a scale of 0–10, where 10 means you 'totally agree' and 0 means you 'totally disagree'. You are free to use any point on the scale to indicate your attitude. However, I urge you to use the mid-point (5) sparingly, if at all. Scores 4 and 6 represent very slight disagreement and agreement respectively. Rarely are we neutral about things so 'close to home'.

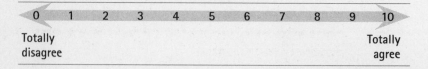

| 0 | 1 | 2 | 3 | 4 | 5 | 6 | 7 | 8 | 9 | 10 |

Totally
disagree

Totally
agree

1. ___ I am comfortable accepting compliments or praise.
2. ___ I give myself the freedom to get things wrong and make mistakes.
3. ___ I find it easy to make clear-cut decisions.
4. ___ I find it easy to relax and am 'comfortable in my own skin'.
5. ___ I set personal development goals.
6. ___ I take action on my goals.

For the remaining items, reverse the scale, so that 0 now means 'Totally agree' and 10 means 'totally disagree'. You are free to use any point on the scale to indicate your attitude, but again I urge you to use the mid-point (5) sparingly, if at all.

0	1	2	3	4	5	6	7	8	9	10

Totally agree   Totally disagree

7. ___ I am frightened of achieving success and coping with it.
8. ___ I fear making a fool of myself.
9. ___ I feel a failure if I don't do a perfect job.
10. ___ I often think I'm not good enough.
11. ___ I am far too tough on myself and my own worst critic.
12. ___ I'm prone to jump to conclusions and later regret it.
13. ___ I often compare myself unfavourably with other people.
14. ___ I tend to rehearse negative outcomes in my head, over and over again.
15. ___ I prefer to stay in my comfort zone and stick with what's familiar.
16. ___ I tend to set myself up for a fall and find a way to mess up before I reach my goal.

17. ___ I speak to myself in a negative way or put myself down in front of others.

18. ___ I avoid taking responsibility so that people don't expect too much of me.

19. ___ I tend to procrastinate.

20. ___ I put my achievements down to luck.

Simply add up the scores for the 20 questions to get your total confidence score.

Total: ___

Scoring

The scores and quiz statements are offered as discussion points to help you to pinpoint the important issues for you and to provide suggestions for what issues to address. This is not a diagnostic test to lumber you with a label, just a starting point to create some signposts.

You also need to consider, what score would be 'good enough' for you? Does anyone have 'perfect confidence' in all situations, at all times and with all people? Most probably not.

- 0–40   indicates low confidence
- 41–80   indicates low to moderate confidence
- 81–120   indicates moderate confidence
- 121–160   indicates moderate to high confidence
- 161–200   indicates high confidence

Relax. Don't worry if your score indicates low or moderate confidence. Remember, we are just at the start of your journey. It's important to focus on what we have and build on it rather than what we have yet to achieve. Think of your existing higher scores on the questions as keyholes. This book is about providing you with the keys to make the most of what you have.

Now let's review the statements in the quiz and consider your higher scores for (positively worded) statements 1–6, and your lower scores for (negatively worded) statements 7–20. These statements represent your strong points.

If you wish you can convert the score from the quiz into an overall rating out of 10. Simply divide your quiz score by 20. Now consider how this compares with the initial rating you made at the start of this chapter. If they are different consider these questions, and write the answers in your journal:

- If your rating scale score is greater than the quiz score, what is it that you know about yourself that the quiz may have overlooked?
- If the quiz score is greater than the rating scale score, what factors has the quiz highlighted that you overlooked for your rating scale?

Now let's consider more closely what a boost in confidence would mean to you.

Your Definition of Confidence

The quiz offers a number of concepts that help define confidence. Some of them may apply to you more than others. For this exercise, write down ten things that contribute to your definition of confidence. With more confidence, what will you be doing that you aren't doing now? State these in terms of positive actions. For instance, instead of 'reduce stress' you would write 'increase relaxation'. Instead of saying 'not be frightened doing' write 'feel comfortable doing'. These will be overall goals to guide the confidence-building process. They represent your future desired confidence outcomes so that the process is more tailor-made to your needs. If you can't think of ten at the moment, you can always return to this exercise as things occur to you. Just to get you started here are some possible statements:

- Confidence for me is being able to talk easily to people I've never met before.
- Confidence for me is being able to pursue a completely new career path.
- Confidence for me is being able to ask someone out for a coffee and feel relaxed or just excited.

	Confidence for me is . . .	Rating
1		
2		
3		
4		
5		
6		
7		
8		
9		
10		

To help you understand where you are now, rate each item from 0 to 10 where 0 equals 'currently not meeting this goal at all' and 10 equals 'totally meeting this goal'. Begin to consider what would need to happen for you to move one point up the scale. Also, what rating would be 'good enough' for each item?

Now let's examine self-esteem.

How's Your Self-Esteem?

Let's define *self-esteem* as an overall evaluation of the feelings you have, either positive or negative, about yourself. This quiz is based on sociologist Morris Rosenberg's test to measure self-esteem. The only change I have made is to alter the measurement scale to match the other tests in this book. Again, the quiz is in two parts and the scoring reverses for the second part. For the first part, rate each of the statements on a scale of 0–10, where 10 means you 'totally agree' with it and 0 means you 'totally disagree'. You are free to use any point on the scale, but once again I urge to use the mid-point (5) sparingly, if at all. Scores 4 and 6 represent very slight disagreement and agreement respectively. Rosenberg's original test didn't even offer the option of neutrality.

1.   I feel that I have a number of good qualities.

0	1	2	3	4	5	6	7	8	9	10

Totally
disagree
Totally
agree

2.   I am able to do things as well as most other people.

0	1	2	3	4	5	6	7	8	9	10

Totally
disagree
Totally
agree

3. I feel that I'm a person of worth, at least on an equal plane with others.

| 0 | 1 | 2 | 3 | 4 | 5 | 6 | 7 | 8 | 9 | 10 |

Totally disagree   Totally agree

4. I take a positive attitude toward myself.

| 0 | 1 | 2 | 3 | 4 | 5 | 6 | 7 | 8 | 9 | 10 |

Totally disagree   Totally agree

5. On the whole, I am satisfied with myself.

| 0 | 1 | 2 | 3 | 4 | 5 | 6 | 7 | 8 | 9 | 10 |

Totally agree   Totally disagree

For the remaining items, reverse the scale, so that 0 means 'totally agree' and 10 means 'totally disagree'. Again, use any point to indicate your attitude but use the mid-point (5) sparingly if at all.

6. At times, I think I am no good at all.

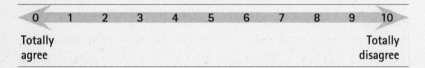

| 0 | 1 | 2 | 3 | 4 | 5 | 6 | 7 | 8 | 9 | 10 |

Totally agree   Totally disagree

7. I feel I do not have much to be proud of.

| 0 | 1 | 2 | 3 | 4 | 5 | 6 | 7 | 8 | 9 | 10 |

Totally agree — Totally disagree

8. I certainly feel useless at times.

| 0 | 1 | 2 | 3 | 4 | 5 | 6 | 7 | 8 | 9 | 10 |

Totally agree — Totally disagree

9. I wish I could have more respect for myself.

| 0 | 1 | 2 | 3 | 4 | 5 | 6 | 7 | 8 | 9 | 10 |

Totally agree — Totally disagree

10. All in all, I am inclined to feel that I am a failure.

| 0 | 1 | 2 | 3 | 4 | 5 | 6 | 7 | 8 | 9 | 10 |

Totally agree — Totally disagree

Scoring

Rosenberg's test only offers a simple mid-way split for scores, that is, high or low self-esteem. I've included five bands, to avoid the simple either/or classification. The best way to interpret these scores is to review the statements in the quiz. Higher scores in the first half of the quiz (items 1–5) indicate higher self-esteem. The reverse is true for the second half (6–10), where lower scores indicate high self-esteem. Reflect on your stronger scores and how you might build on them, even if the overall total is low.

- 0–20   indicates low self-esteem
- 21–40   indicates low to moderate self-esteem
- 41–60   indicates moderate self-esteem
- 61–80   indicates moderate to high self-esteem
- 81–100   indicates high self-esteem

Self-esteem is often about perception and not necessarily about facts. The concept is not without its critics. Therapist and writer Windy Dryden argues that focusing on self-esteem is not productive, as we are ultimately still placing a value on ourselves, even if it's a high one. He argues for the alternative concept of simple self-acceptance where there are no conditions of worth. Perhaps working on esteem issues provides the path to ultimate self-acceptance; when you no longer apply an evaluation (however high), you just accept yourself as you are.

You will have noticed that statements 2 and 3 in the self-esteem quiz involved comparisons to others. So consider, how would your scores change if you removed the comparison?

- I am able to do things well.
- I feel that I'm a person of worth.

What difference does it make? What if you valued yourself by your own standards?

Now that you have a clearer idea about what confidence and esteem mean to you, let's consider a model for personal growth.

The Confidence-Karma Chain Reaction

Mostly we tend to think of our identity as something quite stable and often take it for granted until faced with challenges. Trainer and writer Robert Dilts argues that our sense of identity is subject to a chain of information processing where what happens in our lives, our environment and the people we work with, interacts with other forces, including our feelings, actions and thoughts, values, skills and strengths.

Are you familiar with the executive toy called Newton's Cradle? A row of metal balls hang suspended in a frame. If one ball is pulled away and then let fall to hit the next ball in line, the ball at the furthest end swings out in an arc mirroring the way the first ball dropped. In a similar way changes in one area of your life have a knock-on effect in every other area.

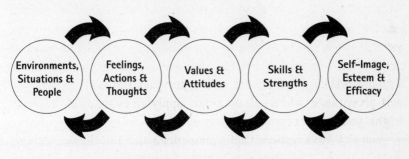

The Confidence-Karma Chain Reaction

If you work along the chain in either direction each link exerts control or influence over the next. Any intervention at any link has a knock-on effect on the other links. So environment (including situations and people) exerts control over our actions (behaviour), thoughts and feelings. In turn these control our values and attitudes and so on. Acquiring a new skill would cause a shift in your self-image (and efficacy), as you would have to see yourself as someone who would be able to gain this new skill. Similarly changes in the way you define yourself have knock-on effects all along the chain, right down to how you deal with people and cope with different environments and new situations. So begin considering the labels you attach to yourself, the way you express your self-image. How do they influence your assessment of your skills and strengths?

Throughout the book we explore all five aspects of the *Confidence-Karma Chain* change process. The exercises, tools and techniques invite you to take action and exert influence. You get to find out at which points the changes have the greatest personal impact. The model also illustrates the karmic process. If we build confidence and esteem in ourselves the knock-on effect means that we influence the environment including other people. If we work on exerting a control over the environment, especially by seeking to build confidence in others, it also has a knock-on effect for our self-image, including our confidence and esteem.

With such a powerful model of change to work with, you can explore your attitudes towards taking action on your confidence-building goals.

Being Ready, Willing and Able

When you think about taking action and doing what it takes to make changes in your life (feelings, thoughts, actions), how ready, willing and able are you? This section aims to find out if there are any barriers to making changes to build confidence, where they lie and what to do to address them.

Readiness

Rate your readiness to make change on a scale of 0–10, where 0 equals 'total unreadiness', where 1 equals the 'first glimmer of readiness' and 10 equals 'all fired up and raring to go'.

0	1	2	3	4	5	6	7	8	9	10
Not ready										Ready

- What tells you that you are at that stage of readiness?
- What have you done to get to this state of readiness?
- If you've rated readiness at 0, what has to happen to create that first glimmer of readiness?
- What number on the scale would you consider a 'good enough' state of readiness to take action?
- What conditions would need to be met to take you up to (or even beyond) 'good enough'?
- What can you do to nudge things in the right direction for you?

Willingness

Rate your willingness to make change on a scale of 0–10, where 0 equals 'totally unwilling', 1 equals the 'first green shoots of willingness' and 10 equals 'willing to do what it takes'.

| 0 | 1 | 2 | 3 | 4 | 5 | 6 | 7 | 8 | 9 | 10 |

Not willing   Willing

- What tells you that you are at that state of willingness?
- What have you done to get to this state of willingness?
- If you've rated readiness at 0, what has to happen to create those first green shoots of willingness?
- What number on the scale would you consider a 'good enough' state of willingness to take action?
- What conditions would need to be met to take you up to (or even beyond) 'good enough'?
- What can you do to nudge things in the right direction for you?

Ability

Do you recognize avenues for change and feel you are able to do something about them? You may be ready to make changes to build confidence, but you may feel that the change in behaviour required is not within your ability. So rate your ability to make changes on a scale of 0–10, where 0 equals 'totally unable', 1 equals the 'first green shoots of willingness' and 10 equals 'totally able'.

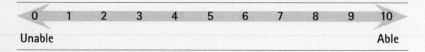

| 0 | 1 | 2 | 3 | 4 | 5 | 6 | 7 | 8 | 9 | 10 |
Unable   Able

- If you've rated readiness at 0, what has to happen to create those first green shoots of willingness?
- What number on the scale would you consider a 'good enough' state of willingness to take action?
- What conditions would need to be met to take you up to (or even beyond) 'good enough'?
- What can you do to nudge things in the right direction for you?

The attitudes of being ready, willing and able tie in with a change formula that informs my coaching practice. I use the concepts of **insight, ownership** and **action**, usually accompanied by the strapline 'It's your life so take it personally'. We may gain the insight that things need to change (readiness), but we then have to take ownership of it (willingness) and then take action on it (ability). The stumbling block often comes at the level of action/ability. Sometimes, we become hypnotized and paralysed by the idea that change takes monumental effort. In reality, there is great significance in the seemingly insignificant. Each little nudge in the right direction has a knock-on effect. This leads us to the principle that often less is most definitely more.

The Pareto Principle

As you work through the book, there will be plenty of opportunities to continue to make small changes which will all add up to something more significant. The Pareto Principle states that 80% of results come from 20% of our efforts; in other words 80% of our efforts bring only modest returns. The cumulative approach in this book offers a way to tap into the 20% that is most meaningful and most effective for you.

Extreme acts of daring are just too far removed from the skills you need in everyday life. So let's consider the more accessible processes and routines that you can use to make changes.

Change Patterns

Part of confidence involves doing something differently or making a change, so pause for a moment to think of the processes you normally go through when faced with the prospect of change. Here are some questions to prompt you:

- What pattern, routine or process do you usually go through to make changes in your life?
- Do you anticipate the need to make changes or do you wait for external forces to put pressure on you?
- What are the steps you go through in your decision-making process?
- In whom would you normally confide when considering making changes?
- What things would you discuss with them when considering change?

Take time to write down these answers. They will reveal the keys to how you cope with change. There's a theory that when we are in danger our lives do flash before our eyes. It's as if our brains are downloading everything we know that may be of use. The problem is that there's just too much information to process. With these questions you have narrowed down to the essentials of how you cope with change. Now you can review these to see what might be self-defeating and what has worked best. This will show you all the actions, feelings and thoughts that contribute to successful change management for you.

Introducing Your One-Minute Promo

Imagine you had to write and deliver a one-minute promotional video presentation of you. The aim is to sell yourself rather than sell yourself short. As you write your script you should be truthful but also consider how best to present yourself in the most favourable light, highlighting your strengths, values and goals. Think about what you have already learned from this chapter about yourself. What thoughts and feelings has it inspired? Think of working through this book and the exercises as the process of gathering background research. For the moment just begin adding raw material. There'll be a chance to edit it later.

Ideas, thoughts and feelings for a One-Minute Promo:

Do something . . .

A key principle in this book is the notion of 'just doing something'. The formula is to start small, review the impact and then either build on the results or, if it doesn't work, try something else. It's a scientific approach to personal development. Sometimes you need to know what doesn't work. It's not a failure, it's just another result, it's feedback.

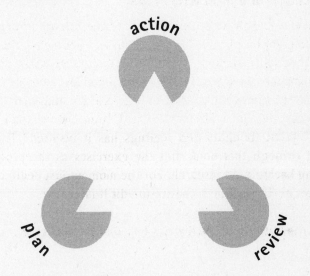

The 'On Par' Learning Triangle

Approach personal development exercises like personal experiments using my **PAR** formula: Plan, Action, Review. Decide what you are going to try, try it, and then review it. Decide whether you need to adjust the plan and then try it again and again. Continue this process until you get the outcome you desire.

What if ...

Before you review what we've covered in this chapter, I'd like you to consider a question that requires a little imagination. It was developed by Insoo Kim Berg and Steve de Shazer and is a key tool in **solution-focused therapy** (and coaching).

Imagine that, after reading this chapter, you go about your day normally and eventually get ready for bed, but when you fall asleep something strange happens. While you are asleep a miracle occurs and you are bestowed with all the confidence you need. The nagging doubts and insecurities have all gone. All your problems with confidence are solved. However, because you are asleep you don't actually know that a miracle has happened. You wake up tomorrow totally unaware that something miraculous happened during the night.

So, as you go about your day, what would be the first signs that would tell you that a miracle has occurred? What else would you do to discover that things have changed for you? How else would your behaviour, feelings and thoughts be different as you begin to realize that a miracle has happened and you have all the confidence you need to take your life forward in positive directions? What would other people around you notice? Take some time to ponder this question thoroughly. Now, of all the things you have considered, what small things could you do right away to contribute to the miracle? What is already happening in your life that is contributing to the miracle?

The essence of the solution-focused approach is always to look for the signs of solution rather than spending time on defining and redefining the problem. So write out your first draft answer and then keep coming back to this scenario and, as thoughts occur to you, keep adding to your miracle picture and keep noticing when bits of it begin to happen.

Review: Finding Your Keys

In this chapter we considered definitions of confidence and esteem through a series of exercises and quizzes. In order to explore how the different aspects of our lives impact on our self-image, we have looked at the *Confidence-Karma Chain*. From the quizzes you have also gained suggestions for confidence and esteem goals. Review your notes and then consider these questions:

- How have these insights impacted on your thoughts and feelings?
- What new insights do you have about being ready, willing and able to take action on confidence-building goals?
- How has it influenced/affected your image of yourself (including esteem and efficacy)?
- What's better for you in terms of confidence?

Your journal or notebook will become a valuable resource, a document of your discoveries and a record of how your confidence grows throughout the journey.

Confidence Rating

What impact has the work you've done in this chapter had on your confidence rating? Use the 0–10 scale, where 0 equals 'no confidence at all' and 10 equals 'total confidence'. You can use fractions of a point if you wish.

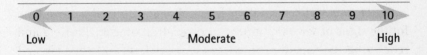

- How far have you progressed along the scale, even if only slightly?

- If you have stayed the same, review the points we've covered and consider in what area of your life you could begin making positive shifts.
- What exercise might it be helpful to repeat?
- What other ideas have you had to boost your confidence rating?
- When will you try this out as a personal experiment?

Karma Call

How do these insights help you to build confidence in others? Write down three affirmative actions you will take to continue the process. What will you pass on to other people in your life? To paraphrase Mahatma Gandhi, 'In order to see changes, what changes will you be?'

1.

2.

3.

In the next chapter, we explore the relationship between the mind and body and the implications for confidence building.

Chapter 2

Confidence Tracking: Looking For What Sparkles and Shines

Look well into thyself; there is a source of strength which will always spring up if thou wilt always look there.

Marcus Aurelius, 121–180, Roman emperor

Preview

This chapter continues the self-evaluation process by considering how your confidence can fluctuate in different environments and the factors that may affect it. It also gets you to consider your skills and strengths and how you can build on them.

The Excluded Middle

Confidence is heavily influenced by context. It's where and with whom you do things and how that makes all the difference. When you let go of the all-or-nothing, black-and-white view of confidence you are free to explore the grey area, the excluded middle, where you can discover your confidence uplifts and confidence downshifts. This chapter is all about looking for what sparkles in your life and where you shine. We often think of personality as a fixed structure but in truth we think, feel and behave as slightly different variations of ourselves with different people and in different situations. That's why we sometimes surprise ourselves by doing something 'out of character'. Once you tease out these confidence highs, you can build on them and borrow from them to use at other times. Confidence building is a transferable skill. As well as passing it on to other people, we can also pass it around to different aspects of ourselves. So let's begin with an assessment of where you are at right now.

Confidence Peaks

If you review your confidence rating in the previous chapter, has there been any movement?

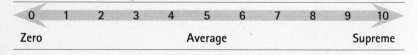

| 0 | 1 | 2 | 3 | 4 | 5 | 6 | 7 | 8 | 9 | 10 |
| Zero | | | | | Average | | | | | Supreme |

- What did you do to create this movement in rating?
- How did you do it?

Essentially this is an average rating. So if you gave a rating of 5, wrapped up in this could be lots of twos, threes, fours, fives, sixes and sevens. Whatever rating you gave, over the duration of working through this book, look out for the moments when your confidence rating peaks above your average score. Make a note of where, when, what, why, who and how in your journal.

- Where are you?
- When does it happen?
- What are you doing to create this peak?
- Who is with you?
- What skills can you borrow from this situation to help in other areas of your life?
- When, where and with whom are you most relaxed?
- When, where and with whom are you most 'your self'?

Looking for What Sparkles

When coaching clients, I often begin the process by asking them a few general background questions. I do this not just to gain a sense about the client's personal context, but also to create a relaxed environment by getting the client to consider things that relax them. These questions also tap into people's strengths. Here are some similar questions for you to answer:

1. What do you enjoy doing in your spare time?
2. What hobbies, pastimes, and sports to do you enjoy?
3. How do you like to relax?
4. With whom do you enjoy spending your time?
5. What are you favourite places to visit?

Spend a few moments considering these questions and write down as many things as you can (here or in your journal).

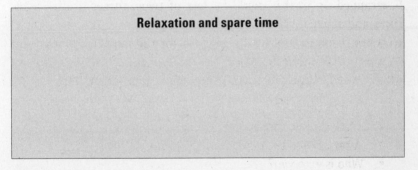

Relaxation and spare time

These questions may help you to tap into what 'sparkles and shines' for you. Nothing is insignificant in confidence building. Every sparkle is a start. The ability to relax, have fun and enjoy yourself is a cornerstone of confidence, so don't underestimate the power of these questions.

Now let's consider different areas of your life and explore how these influence your confidence rating.

Life Spheres

Far from us having just one, fixed, unwavering personality, our personality is made up of a number of variations on a central theme that we employ in different aspects of our lives depending on the roles we play. Below I've listed the major areas common to every person's life. For each one, rate how confident you feel operating within it, using a rating from 0 to 10, where 0 is not all confident and 10 is supremely confident.

Family life ____   Work life ____   Social life ____   Leisure time ____

- Where do things sparkle? Where do you shine?
- In what areas of life are your higher scores?
- What do you do in these areas that make this higher score?
- What other factors contribute to this higher score?
- What could you take from one context, however small, and use in another?
- Is there another area of your life you could consider? What rating would you give it?

Other areas not included above (and their rating)

Now let's look at the different roles we play in life to explore what sparkles and shines there.

Life Roles

Here are some of our life roles for the different spheres. These roles are shaped by the environment and determined by our interactions with others. Consider which of these apply to you and give each of them a confidence rating using the above 0–10 scale.

Partner ____	Parent ____	Child ____	Sibling ____
Customer ____	Client ____	Friend ____	Opponent ____
Colleague ____	Employee ____	Employer ____	Supervisor ____
Neighbour ____	Lover ____	Subordinate ____	Leader ____
Assistant ____	Advisor ____	Consultant ____	Patient ____

- Examining your scores, where are your highest ratings?
- How do you do that?
- What makes these scores higher than your average score?
- Which roles are bringing out the best in you? How come? What are you doing in these roles that you're not in others?
- What can you borrow from your high-scoring roles and apply to others?
- If you could think of one tiny thing that you do in these roles that gives you higher than average scores, what would it be?
- Are there other roles you'd like to consider in which you have high confidence ratings?

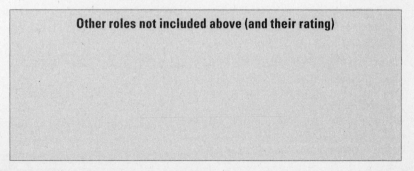

Other roles not included above (and their rating)

Now let's consider different types of people in your life.

Different People

Listed below are various types of people you may interact with in your life. Focusing only on those people you actually do interact with, rate your confidence using the 0–10 scale. Feel free to add other people in your life not on this list.

Your partner ____	Family ____	Friends ____	Acquaintances ____
Colleagues ____	Strangers ____	Shopkeepers ____	Children ____
Parents ____	Religious figures ____	Younger people ____	Older people ____
People from other cultures ____	Members of a club ____	Peers ____	Employer ____
Employees ____	Staff ____	Clients ____	Customers ____
Cold-callers ____	Salespeople ____	Your doctor ____	Nurses ____
Your dentist ____	Bank tellers ____	Solicitors ____	Neighbours ____

Again, examine your scores and note the ones above your average confidence rating. Next take time to consider and write down the answers to these questions:

- With whom do you shine?
- What is it about how you behave with these people that contributes to the higher score?
- What other factors contribute to this higher score?
- What behaviours from the higher-scoring interactions could you apply to other relationships?
- Is there another person in your life you could consider with whom your confidence scores are higher? What is your rating?

Another person not mentioned above (and their rating)

Continuing this line of thought, let's now consider how different situations impact on your confidence ratings.

Different Situations

We interact with the various people in our lives in our different roles and other factors influence our behaviour so that two encounters may never be exactly the same. On the way to work you might have to deal with a rude shopkeeper. You may get stuck in a traffic jam. You might meet someone who pays you a compliment. It might be sunny; it might rain. You may have had a great night's sleep or suffered a bout of insomnia. You might have a great new hairstyle or may be having a bad hair day. Sometimes small changes can have a dramatic effect on our mood. The same applies to confidence.

Write a brief statement indicating your ideal conditions for maximum confidence based on your life experience so far. What constitutes a good day, in terms of your confidence?

My conditions for higher confidence are:

When all of these ideal conditions are in place, how would you rate your confidence on a scale from 0 to 10, where 0 equals 'none at all', 1 or 2 represent 'a small glimmer of confidence' and 10 equals 'dazzling confidence'.

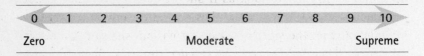

| 0 | 1 | 2 | 3 | 4 | 5 | 6 | 7 | 8 | 9 | 10 |

Zero · · · · · · · · Moderate · · · · · · · Supreme

Now consider what conditions have already been met and how you will you build on these.

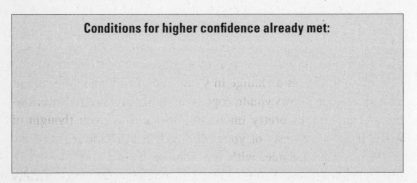

Conditions for higher confidence already met:

Case Study: Model Mode

One client, let's call her Michelle, came to me for confidence coaching. She claimed to 'go to pieces' in social situations and 'turn into a gibbering wreck'. She also avoided job interviews although she was well qualified to apply for a number of different positions. I began by asking her what she liked doing in her spare time. She immediately became animated and more alive. Her face 'lit up' when she talked about fashion. This was clearly an area of 'sparkle and shine' for Michelle. She told me that she had attended model casting, which sounded to me like quite an intimidating experience. In a casting lots of people try out for a modelling job and have to walk up and down a room in front of judges and highly competitive strangers. When I asked Michelle how she managed to get through it, she said, 'Oh, mostly it's just a trick. I just switch into model mode.' I asked her to show me. Suddenly her whole demeanour transformed. Model mode is the mindset she uses that allows her to look as if she belongs there. She changes her whole body language and takes on a different persona. When I commented on the startling transformation, she said 'Oh but it's all a trick.' Then I asked how she learned the trick. She told me she had picked it up by observing how other models behaved and then practised at home in front of the mirror.

Acknowledging and complimenting a client on their own successes is a key part of coaching, mainly because we often forget to do it for ourselves. I said to Michelle: 'You taught yourself and perfected a technique that changes your mood and mindset and immediately causes a change in your whole body and demeanour. This technique allows you to cope in a highly pressurized environment. That sounds pretty impressive to me. Have you thought of using it in other areas of your life?' When Michelle realized she could use model mode, with the volume turned down to match different situations, things started to change quite dramatically for her. She now has a job she loves and is the life and soul of many different work and social situations. Over four sessions we worked on her self-evaluation to underpin the change in perception.

One-Minute Promo

What new information can you add to the background research for your one-minute promo?

Now let's journey further into your confidence landscape, using the SWOT technique originally devised to evaluate business projects. It was developed by Albert Humphrey, a business and management consultant working at the Stanford Research Institute. You can also apply it to confidence building.

SWOT Your Confidence

SWOT stands for: **Strengths, Weaknesses, Opportunities, Threats.** This method can help us quickly to pinpoint our assets and limitations. Each section comprises several questions that you can answer from three perspectives: your own, someone close to you, and a 'fly-on-the-wall' objective observer. Use a separate page for each section. You may also use this exercise and these questions with other people, remembering that the aim is to draw out information not to impose ideas.

Strengths

Take your time to reflect on each of the questions below. Each question takes a slightly different angle and they are designed to help you to tease out a list of strengths based on your life experience.

- Knowing yourself as you do, what's pushing you forward?
- What strengths do you have to advance your personal and professional development?
- What skills and strengths do you have to build confidence in your life and in the lives of others?
- Knowing yourself as you do, what gives you an advantage, an edge or a head start?
- Thinking of a personal achievement, what skills and strengths did you call upon?
- Thinking of a time when you helped someone out of a difficult situation, what strengths and skills did you use?

- Thinking of a personal problem you solved or an obstacle you overcame, what strengths and skills brought you through?
- Knowing yourself as you do, what skills and strengths do you sometimes overlook or dismiss?
- Anything else? What other skills and strengths do you possess?

Don't be in a rush to hurry through the questions. Sometimes we need that extra prompt and extra thinking time to dig deeper.

Now consider how someone close to you (friend, family, partner, etc.) might answer the questions. Then consider an objective observer. What would they say your strengths are?

Someone close:	Objective observer:

Exercise

What would constitute a 'strong week' ahead for you, one where you are using your key strengths? Draft out your strong-week plan. Do this at the beginning of each week, adding new strengths you have uncovered.

Weaknesses

The purpose of these questions is not to drag you down – it's important for us all to get used to anticipating the impact our limitations may have. Again answer the questions in terms of your own personal development, particularly confidence building, and from the perspectives of someone close to you and of an objective observer.

- Knowing yourself as you do, what's holding you back?
- What limitations (weaknesses) sometimes hinder you in achieving your goal or building your confidence?
- Knowing yourself as you do, what limitations do you place on yourself?
- What limitations hinder or slow down your personal and professional development, including confidence building?
- After reconsidering your strengths, which limitations don't really matter as much as you first thought?
- Knowing yourself as you do, how can you manage your limitations most productively?
- What skills and strengths do you have to address some of your limitations?

Now consider how someone close to you (friend, family, partner, etc.) might answer the questions. Then consider the viewpoint of an objective observer.

Someone close:	Objective observer:

In recent years there has been a shift towards thinking about maximizing our strengths rather than obsessing about eradicating weaknesses. We can't be expected to be absolutely fabulous at absolutely everything. It is essential we are selective. We expand on what we are good at and manage those things we are not so good at. We either improve enough to get by or form a partnership with someone who complements our strengths (and vice versa). Can you use your strengths in a more creative way? Can you use different situations and contexts to reduce the impact of your limitations?

Opportunities

A key part of confidence building is to recognize opportunities and take action to seize them. Take a moment to review the exercises on 'Life Spheres', 'Life Roles', and 'Different People' before considering these questions.

- Knowing yourself as you do, what opportunities, resources and choices do you have to focus on personal and professional development, particularly confidence building?
- How will you maximize these opportunities?
- What environmental factors or situations support or enhance your personal and professional development, including confidence building?
- What opportunities are there to help you minimize your limitations?
- How do present (or future) opportunities support your strengths?
- What opportunities do you have to build and boost confidence in other people?
- Anything else? What other opportunities may you be overlooking?

Now consider how someone close to you (friend, family, partner, etc.) might answer the questions. Then consider the viewpoint of an objective observer. What would they say your opportunities are?

Someone close:	Objective observer:

Threats

A key strategy in personal development, goal setting and confidence building is to consider possible threats and obstacles from the outset, and what strengths and resources you already have to deal with them.

- What's getting in the way of your confidence building?
- What are the threats that may thwart your personal and professional development and growth?
- What strengths and opportunities do you have to help minimize threats to your confidence building?
- What threats might reveal your limitations and what resources can you call on to defend against these threats?
- What situations and environmental factors are obstacles to your development and growth?
- What's holding you back from building and boosting your own confidence?
- What's holding you back from building and boosting confidence in others?

Now consider how someone close to you (friend, family, partner, etc.) might answer the questions. Then consider the viewpoint of an objective observer. What would they say your strengths are in helping you to deal with threats?

Someone close:	Objective observer:

Prompt for Strengths

Here's a prompt list for strengths. Circle as many as apply to you.

realism	persuasion	communication	bravery
logic	creativity	organization	empathy
listening	influence	imagination	flexibility
courage	optimism	decisiveness	persistence
solution-finding	purposefulness	calmness	adaptability

For the items you've circled, ask yourself these questions:

- In what ways have I demonstrated _____, in words and deeds in the past month?
- In what ways have I demonstrated _____, in words and deeds in the past week?
- In what ways have I demonstrated _____, in words and deeds today?

Repeat these questions for your strengths from previous exercises.

Exercise

From your list of top strengths, select up to ten. Write each strength on a separate slip of paper. Now place them in order. This is your strengths hierarchy. Select the top three and decide what immediate actions you can take to support them. Repeat this exercise each week.

Making the Most of What You Have

So are you really using your strengths and skills and maximizing your opportunities? Consider these two rating scales and supplementary questions.

Using Strengths

Rate the extent to which you are currently using your strengths, where 0 equals not at all and 10 equals totally.

0	1	2	3	4	5	6	7	8	9	10
Not at all					Moderately					Totally

- How have you got this far along the scale?
- What is it that has helped you to get from 0 to where you are now?
- What can you imagine doing if you move one point up the scale?
- What small, significant action will you take to make use of your strengths over the coming week to further your personal development?

Maximizing Opportunities

Rate the extent to which you are currently maximizing your opportunities, where 0 equals not at all and 10 equals totally.

0	1	2	3	4	5	6	7	8	9	10
Not at all					Moderately					Totally

- How have you got this far along the scale?
- What is it that has helped you to get from 0 to where you are now?

- What can you imagine doing if you move one point up the scale?
- What opportunity, however small, will you seize over the coming week to further your personal development?

Good Enough?

Often with coaching clients this approach comes as a revelation. They realize that they don't necessarily need to score a 'perfect ten'. In university exams, 'good enough to pass' is often 40%. To get an A grade it's usually 70%. To achieve an exceptional A*, it's 80%. This puts the 'good enough' range between 4 and 7 out of ten (or 8/10 if you want to be exceptional). Of course, it's good to push for excellence, but it's equally important to keep things in perspective.

1. What will represent 'good enough' for you? What number on the scale?
2. How will you know when you get there? What will you be doing differently to what you're doing now?

Also, when comparing where you are now with 'what's good enough' you may realize you don't have as far to go as you originally thought. If you score a 4 for where you are now, and if 7 is 'good enough' (instead of 10) then you are more than halfway there.

Being in the Mood & Getting in the Mood

One common reason for delaying action is 'not being in the mood'. In emergency situations we don't wait to get in the mood. We just do whatever needs to be done. Wrapped up in the 'not in the mood' script are a whole host of thoughts and feelings. Often we spend more time and energy avoiding the task than just doing it. So consider if you are putting off doing things that could help you build and boost your confidence.

Get a sheet of paper, or use your journal. At the top write a situation that you are avoiding, or delaying through procrastination.

Now draw a line down the middle of the paper. On the left-hand side make a list of all the thoughts that you use to persuade yourself to delay taking action. Now, on the right-hand side, make a list of the thoughts that motivate you to take action.

Task/Situation that you're delaying or waiting to be in the mood to take action on:	
Thoughts delaying action:	Thoughts promoting action:

Spend longer on the thoughts promoting action. Pay attention to those that cancel out items on the delay list. For instance, in the left-hand delay list you might put 'stress'. You may well find the thought of action stressful. However, balance this with the fact that procrastination causes stress. Often we take action when the stress of delaying it becomes greater than the stress of doing it. Doing it more quickly could save you a lot of stress. When you have listed ten or more reasons on the 'promoting action' side, pick the three most compelling reasons to take action, and just do it.

Now consider three benefits of giving up the procrastination habit. What will you gain?

1.

2.

3.

Review all of the exercises from this chapter and make a list of your strengths and opportunities for personal development on a separate piece of paper and carry it around with you. Review it regularly, especially first thing in the morning and last thing at night. The idea is really to internalize the list so you are primed to seize opportunities and use your strengths when situations arise.

My strengths are:	My opportunities are:

Also, make up a series of small notes, each with a different one of your top ten strengths, and place them in prominent places in your home and at work to serve as reminders.

In the next exercise we consider the power and impact of labels.

Black and White Categories

Circle one item in each pair that you feel best describes you.

Powerful/ Powerless	Controlling/ Controlled	Logical/ Emotional	Dominant/ Submissive
Tough/Tender	Warm/Cold	Strong/Weak	Active/Passive
Winner/Loser	Lucky/Unlucky	Winner/Quitter	Walker/Talker
Sensitive/ Insensitive	Assertive/ Unassertive	Kind/Cruel	Good/Bad

Optimist/	Tactful/	Leader/Follower	Somebody/
Pessimist	Tactless		Nobody

Consider how each of these labels affects your view of your skills and your strengths. How would things be different if you had chosen the opposite label in the pair? What if you were able to pick a label from 'the grey' area between these two polar opposites? How would this affect your view of your skills and strengths?

Keep exploring the grey areas, the excluded middle, for what shines and sparkles in your life and how you can build on these skills, strengths and insights. Keep observing what happens in your life that has a positive impact on your confidence. What are you doing? Where are you? How are you achieving this confidence peak? What else is helping? Who is helping? These insights will also be useful for goal setting in all areas of your life.

Something Else for the One-Minute Promo

Thoughts feelings, attitudes and action:

Review: Finding Your Keys

Review the *Confidence-Karma Chain* in Chapter 1 to see how the things we have considered in this chapter relate to other aspects of confidence building. This chapter has focused on the link in the chain to do with environment, other people and situations, as well as skills and strengths. You may also wish to go through the full

review process from Chapter 1, or just take the shorter version.
Either way, review the results from the exercises and consider:

- How do you rate your confidence at the conclusion of this chapter?
- What's better for you in terms of confidence?
- What have been the most effective aspects of this chapter in taking you forward?
- What knock-on effects do you imagine there will be if you put the information in this chapter into practice?

Karma Call

Consider how these new insights can help you to build confidence in others. Write down three affirmative actions you will take to continue the process. What will you pass on to other people in your life? 'In order to see changes, what changes will you be?'

1.

2.

3.

Chapter 3

Mindful and Bodywise

The mind of the sage, being in repose, becomes the mirror of
the universe, the speculum of all creation.

Zhuang Zhou, 369–286 BCE, philosopher

Preview

In this chapter we explore the mind–body connection, in particular
relaxation, the master key to unlocking your confidence . You will find
various exercises to help you control stress, get in touch with your
body and consider the impact of your health on confidence building

---

Being Still

An indispensable part of the psychology of peak performance and
confidence building is the ability to take control of our mental
states, and relax. Philosopher Laozi stated, 'To the mind that is still,
the whole universe surrenders.' True confidence begins with stillness. Proceeding from this basis we can build on skills, strengths
and opportunities. In this chapter we explore and experience the
interaction between our physical being and our mental states and
how we can use one to control the other for positive outcomes.
Essentially, in this chapter you'll learn how to **Stun STAN** (Stress,
Tension, Anxiety and Nervousness) and induce relaxation as a solid
basis for building confidence. We consider practical techniques for
taking control of your relaxation response and focusing awareness,
and the theory behind them, principally the mind–body connection

and mindfulness. Let's begin by briefly considering the basic learning principles on which the techniques are based.

ACE Learning

Basically, we learn everything in three main ways, that is, by associations, by consequences and by example.

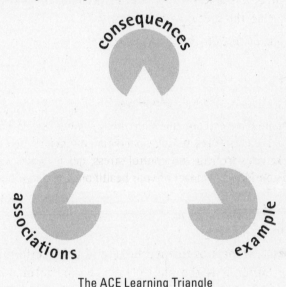

The ACE Learning Triangle

Associations

We learn by making links and associations between objects, ideas, thoughts, feelings, emotional states and events. In psychology this is known as **classical conditioning**, and the most famous example was researcher Ivan Pavlov's (somewhat cruel) experiments with dogs. Pavlov rang a bell immediately before feeding a group of dogs. For the dogs, food became associated with a ringing bell to the extent that they would salivate merely at the sound of the bell. We humans can do the same thing when we see photographs of food or even read a description of a delicious meal. We have also learned to associate abstract collections of symbols (words) with physical objects. That's how we learn to read. The associations don't necessarily have to be meaningful; the links can be made merely by events repeatedly occurring at the same time.

Consequences

We tend to repeat behaviours that have positive consequences and avoid those that don't. Our behaviour is shaped by rewards and punishments, pleasure and pain. In psychology this is known as **operant conditioning**. The principle of 'learning by consequence' shapes our behaviour. It's a matter of trial and error. Continually we make changes in line with the feedback until we meet a target. This is how babies learn to walk, how we learn to ride a bike, learn a new language or just about anything. Overall, psychological research shows that reward works better than punishment. It is far more effective to reward those behaviours we want repeated and ignore the behaviours we want to go away. So you really should ignore your screaming child in the supermarket. Don't give them sweets to shut them up. They see this as a reward for crying. Instead reward them when they actually shut up.

Example

We also learn by observing other people. Any action we observe in others and attempt to imitate is known in psychology as **modelling**. It also lets us observe the consequences of actions without having to test them out for ourselves. This is called **vicarious learning**. Soap operas appeal to us because we get to discuss real-world moral dilemmas without having to put ourselves in those situations.

Taken together we've learned just about everything in our lives by these three methods (ACE) and you will be able to learn the techniques in this chapter by the same principles.

The Mind–Body Connection

The mind–body connection has fascinated philosophers, poets and scientists for millennia. In everyday language we credit both mental and physical events with the power to cause change. We talk about psychosomatic illnesses or 'mind over matter'. We also use bodily metaphors for emotional responses. So fear is equated with a loss of bowel function and extreme humour with a failing bladder. The eyes are the windows to the soul. The heart is the seat of emotions. We get butterflies in the stomach. We describe other people as 'a pain in the neck' (or worse). We clap our hands to show appreciation. When we begin something challenging we take a deep breath. When we wake up first thing in the morning we stretch.

Yoga brings together the dual aims of strengthening the body and quietening the mind and is supported by physiological psychology. Our pattern-seeking brains look to establish a congruent, harmonious relationship between body and mind. Mental moods and physical states seek to match each other. Research shows that by controlling our physical body we can influence our mental state. We can exploit this relationship by deliberately changing our posture to give our brain cues to change our moods.

Exercise

Change your posture now. Slump in the chair, drop your shoulders, let your body go listless and put a 'down-at-heel, hang-dog' expression on your face. Act as if your body has just become heavy and it's an effort to lift your limbs. Let out exasperated sighs. As you continue you will find that your mental state begins to match your body language. Now reverse this by sitting up straight or, better still, stand up and stretch. Chin up, chest out, stomach in and stretch your hands up to the sky and smile. Take long, deep, energizing breaths. Keep doing this and you will notice another shift in energy as mind and body begin to synchronize.

Breathing is the key to changing our physiological responses. If we are facing a tough challenge, we naturally take a deep breath to steady our nerves. Deep breathing has a calming effect on the mind and body. In times of stress we hold our breath or breathe more shallowly; we also match this by holding on too tightly to our bodies, getting knots of tension in the shoulders, and stomach pains. Interestingly, the literal meaning of 'inspire' is to breathe in. Inspiration comes before significant action. Top athletes know this and employ a strategic approach to relaxation. Their drive to push the physical limits of the human body begins on a solid foundation of relaxation and stress control. Relaxation is not a luxury. It's essential.

Being Brainy

Brain cells, known as neurons, are tiny information transmitters and processors. Some gather information (sensory neurons), some control physical movement (motor neurons) and about a billion neurons in between handle perception, learning, remembering, decision making and controlling complex behaviours. As we learn we create neural pathways, brain connections, rather like the footpaths across a field. The greater the traffic over the track, the more defined the path becomes. Regular practice reinforces the new learning in the brain. It's the same whether we're learning to ride a bike, learning to play a musical instrument or practising meditation and breathing techniques.

The more we do it the more profound are the effects. Strategic control of your breathing and relaxation response changes your nervous system. Our brains respond immediately to our efforts. When we are awake and alert our brain produces beta waves and when we are relaxed it produces alpha waves. Simply by closing your eyes and taking a deep breath, more alpha wave activity is generated in the brain. This is enough for our pattern-seeking, congruence-loving brain to respond, and more changes follow. Altering your bodily state with deep breathing is a way of short-circuiting the stress response. If your brain receives the signals that the body is relaxed, it seeks to complete the process and calm the mind (and vice versa). We cannot be anxious and relaxed at the same time. Much of this chapter is about using these techniques consciously and strategically to control stress by triggering relaxation.

Stress

Stress is more than just a collection of physiological responses. A key factor is individual perception as we make sense of environmental and psychological demands. Essentially we feel stressed when we feel out of control, that is when the perceived demands upon us outweigh our perceived capability to deal with them. The physical responses are pretty much the same for everyone. Perception creates the difference.

We generally think of stress as a bad thing, but we all need a moderate amount of stress to bring out the best in our performance. Some of us thrive on that little adrenaline rush. It gives us an edge. However, there's a tipping point at which the effect reverses. Moderate amounts of stress sharpen our performance but too much dulls it. This fine line makes it imperative for us to exercise control over our responses to stress. We can do this psychologically by altering our perception of it. We can also take control of our stress responses physically, by breathing and relaxation techniques.

Fight or Flight

When something triggers our stress response, it puts us in alarm mode. It's known as the fight-or-flight response. Simply put, we either tackle the stress 'head on' or we 'run for cover'. The brain gets busy and fires off impulses to the nervous system which set off a whole chain reaction of changes. Our hearts beat faster, our breathing quickens, our blood sugar level increases and we sweat. Pupils in the eyes become wider. Hormones are released to continue these responses, such as adrenaline. Other hormones maintain the responses.

Now it's interesting to consider that these responses occur when we see someone we really fancy as well as when we are scared. So, depending on our perception, we can process these responses as a threat or just a rush. If it's a threat we either approach to deal with it or avoid it. If it's perceived as a rush we can use it to enhance performance. Fight or flight doesn't mean we have to go up and punch someone on the nose. We could approach them and say 'hello' (or run off and hide in the toilets). When applied to confidence building, two factors are important: the interpretation of physical changes; and the ability to keep these changes within productive limits.

Stress creates a physical and mental state of readiness. You'll recall that attitudes were defined in similar terms in the Introduction. Attitudes frame our perceptions of the world. So you can either take action and use the energy boost, or else continue in a state of alarm and allow it to overwhelm you. For most people, the bodily responses to alarm are short-lived and soon return to normal. The problems associated with stress occur when this state of readiness persists and depletes the body's resources. Maintaining high adrenaline levels compromises the body's immune system, leaving us less able to ward off attack from bacteria and viruses. Eventually stress leads to exhaustion with disturbed eating patterns (over- and under-eating). In extreme cases, chronic (long-term) stress leads to psychological problems with anger and aggression (fight) in some people, but results in apathy and depression (flight) in others. Research has shown that physical health problems associated with long-term stress include asthma, colitis, ulcers, cancer and heart attacks. So it makes good sense to do what we can to protect ourselves.

One notable symptom of stress is that breathing tends to be shallower. When we are relaxed we tend to breathe more deeply and fully. By taking control of our breathing patterns we exploit and enjoy the vital connection that exists between our minds and our bodies.

Type A and Type B Confidence

Heart specialists Meyer Friedman and Ray Rosehan examined the links between patterns of behaviour and health, in particular with respect to the incidence of heart disease. Their findings indicated two broad types of behavioural patterns: Type A and Type B. The Type A people live their lives like coiled springs. They are 'driven', ambitious, competitive, alert, impatient and aggressive. Not surprisingly they are more prone to stress. In contrast Type B people do not appear so 'driven'. Although often equally ambitious, they are less likely to shout about it and allow it to dominate their lives. They choose leisure pursuits that are less competitive. Type Bs are what we might call better 'people people' and tend to balance time for 'ambition' with time for family and friends. Research has shown that holding hands helps to calm nerves, and showing affection, such as by hugging, releases the brain chemical oxytocin (described as the love hormone). This also reduces stress and is being explored as a way of treating depression. Positive feelings have a beneficial effect on heart health. By comparison, people exhibiting Type A behaviour are more than two and a half times more likely to develop heart disease than those showing Type B behaviour. Of the two types, it is Type A people who are more likely to be perceived as confident. However, it's not confidence if it gives you a heart attack!

Hassles and Uplifts

We often associate stress with major life events such as a change of job, ill heath, the break up of a relationship or the loss of a loved one. These events can overwhelm us. However, there is another theory that it's the little things in life that stack up to create stress. We go through each day experiencing small hassles and small uplifts. At the end of the day, if the hassles outweigh the uplifts we conclude it's been a bad day. If the uplifts outweigh the hassles we call it a good day. According to this view, if we focus on boosting the number of uplifts, we can cancel out the hassles and balance the day. What are your daily uplifts? Take a moment to write them down now and, more importantly, make them happen more often.

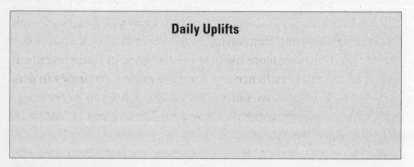

Daily Uplifts

Broaden and Build

Stress puts us into survival mode and narrows our focus. The fight-or-flight response is not an expansive state, it's a knee-jerk, black-and-white state prompting a narrow range of survival-directed behaviours. This limited range of options quickens our response time. We don't have to search our minds for the appropriate reaction. So, if we live our lives in perpetual stress, we narrow our options. In survival mode our minds become closed off to new learning experiences and we react in an almost robotic manner. Overall, we learn more effectively when we are relaxed and not locking out new information. The **broaden-and-build theory of positive emotions** argues that cultivating positive emotions broadens our awareness and encourages learning. It was developed by Positive Psychologist Barbara Fredrickson. Its key insight is the understanding that in positive states we can entertain and explore new and varied feelings, actions and thoughts.

This theory has important implications for confidence building. Although positive emotions do not necessarily have an immediate survival benefit, the additional skills and resources we build by broadening our options enhance survival. Friendships often begin from a greeting, sharing a joke or a bit of small-talk. This develops our social network. Grandparents know that playing with grand-children provides a lot more exercise than they were previously used to. This may lead to improvements in health and energy levels. Also, spending time cultivating positive emotions changes our perception so that we more likely to see the good in future events. It also helps to build resilience and improve coping strategies to deal with life's challenges by putting negative emotional experiences into a much broader context. Higher resilience leads to improved well-being and happiness.

Research has shown that cultivating positive emotions can help improve flexible thinking and openness to new information, memory, moral reasoning and relationships. Whereas stress can cause a downward spiral of fatigue, anxiety and depression, the broaden-and-build theory suggests that we can create an upward spiral of well-being.

In Chapter 8 we'll look at a broaden-and-build based visual-ization, but in the meantime here's an exercise to begin retuning your perception to positive feelings. Research has shown that adopting a positive mental attitude may lower the risk of a heart attack. That alone has to be reason enough to try it.

Exercise: Getting the Gratitude Attitude

Keep your journal or notebook by the side of your bed. Each evening reflect on your day and write down three things for which you are grateful. They don't have to be earth-shattering events. You could extend this and write down three people to whom you were grateful that day. This exercise means you go to sleep with positive feelings. The next morning, write down three things you are looking forward to that day, however small. This sets up positive anticipations for the day. This exercise helps to retune your perceptions so that you don't overlook the good stuff. Do it every day for a month and assess the effects.

Every Breath You Take

Breathing is something we take for granted simply because it seems to take care of itself. However, many of us generally do not use the full capacity of our lungs. When we are stressed our breathing becomes even shallower. By contrast when we are relaxed, happy and contented our breathing becomes fuller and deeper. Due to gravity, the lower part of the lungs has the greatest blood supply. This means that fuller, deeper breathing helps to reduce the number of breaths we take and is more efficient at oxygenating the blood. The heart doesn't have to work as hard and blood pressure doesn't need to be so high. Deep breathing uses the abdominal muscles and the diaphragm, a large muscle between the lungs and the abdomen, to help fully inflate the longs. This also has a massaging effect on the internal organs, which improves blood flow and detoxification. If this isn't enough, research has indicated that controlled breathing slows down the heart rate, normalizes blood pressure, improves digestion, increases energy and improves cognitive functions. A knock-on effect is that it may even make sex more enjoyable. Surely this sounds like a great recipe for confidence? Since we have to breathe anyway it is one of few things in life that yields such a big return on such a minor investment.

Mindfulness

The concept of mindfulness is found in many different spiritual traditions and is particularly associated with Buddhism. However, in recent years it has gained a secular appeal and has found its way into therapy, coaching training and the self-help movement. In a nutshell, mindfulness is just about paying attention in a particular way. It's about present-moment awareness and attending to the here and now without judgement. Once we begin to judge something it takes us out of the present moment. We stop observing and start commentating. Buddhism advocates that we should apply mindfulness in our everyday lives by maintaining calm, present-moment awareness of our bodies, sensations, feelings, thoughts, perceptions and consciousness. Mindfulness can take many forms. For example, as well as the mindfulness of breathing, we can also practise mindfulness of the body, stopping and resting, and scanning our body's response.

According to new research, when we practise mindfulness-based meditation programmes the active areas of the brain are those associated with learning, memory, developing and appreciating different perspectives and processing information related to the self. Stress narrows our focus. Relaxation helps to shift the emphasis away from the survival-focused 'me me me'. Mindfulness is the foundation on which we can broaden and build.

Here's a basic mindfulness technique to begin with.

Cultivating Stillness

Close your eyes, take long slow deep breaths and simply focus your attention on your breath. If an intrusive thought pops into your mind, just acknowledge the beginning of the thought and then observe when it ends. Then bring your attention back to monitoring your breathing. That's all. If you want you can name the thought and then let it go. You will notice that the thoughts become less frequent and the periods of stillness increase.

Now let's consider some basic deep-breathing techniques.

Basic Abdominal Breathing

This breathing technique forms the basis for much of this chapter and for the visualization techniques in Chapter 8. Try this:

- Sit down with your back straight and feet firmly on the floor. Get comfortable.
- Now focus your attention on your breathing.
- Begin by taking long slow deep breaths, in through your nose and out through your mouth.
- As you breathe in, let the air expand your lungs as fully as possible by letting your abdomen expand.
- As you breathe out, slowly bring in your abdomen (the area around your navel) to squeeze out the air. Do this slowly and gently. Don't strain. The whole process should be smooth and relaxing.
- If at any time your mind wanders or thoughts pop into your head, simply acknowledge these thoughts and let them go. Just keep bringing your attention back to your breathing.
- Do this for ten breaths.

Let's take this a step further and introduce the idea of counting to regulate your breathing. This technique also includes an instruction to hold your breath. However, your own knowledge of your medical history, plus just your sense of comfort should override this if necessary. So if you have any respiratory problems, blood-pressure problems, heart problems or any other medical condition, then consult your doctor. If you are in this situation omit the breath-holding instructions in this book for the meantime and just pause for a moment.

Count and Hold Abdominal Breathing

Think of this as a training exercise to deepen your breathing.

- Begin as with the previous technique, sitting comfortably with your back straight and feet on the floor. Breathe in through the nose and out through the mouth.
- Focus your attention on your breath.
- Breathe in and let the air expand your lungs as fully as possible by letting your abdomen expand.
- Breathe out, slowly bringing in your abdomen (the area around your navel) to squeeze out the air.
- Now begin to regulate your breathing by a count of 8:4:8. (If you can't manage this, try 6:3:6 or 4:2:4).
- Breathe in to the mental count of 8.
- Hold for the mental count of 4.
- Breathe out to the mental count of 8.
- If at any time thoughts pop into your head, don't fight them or resent them, just acknowledge them and let them drift away. Keep bringing your mind back to your breathing, gently.
- Do this for ten breaths.

Two-Minute Stress-Buster

This is a favourite technique of mine. It was developed as a challenge to people who say they just don't have time to 'mess about' with relaxation exercises. I maintain that if you can't take two minutes, three times a day, to do this little exercise then it's high time you looked at your life balance and time management. Here it is:

- Stand upright with your feet shoulder width apart, head up and eyes closed and do seven counted abdominal breaths.
- Breathe in fully through your nose and smile.
- Hold for the mental count of four
- Breathe out through your mouth and say 'aaaaaah' in the form of a sigh.
- Do this seven to ten times.

Do this three times throughout the day. Every hour on the hour would be even better. If you are not able to do this exercise in private, just say 'aaaah' in your imagination. After a week of doing the exercise, review it. How is it working for you? When are the best times for you?

Meditation is a Walk in the Park

We use the phrase 'a walk in the park' to describe something that's easy to do. So, some time this week, make an appointment with yourself in your diary to go for a walk in the park, or a walk in nature. The aim is just to experience the moment not to analyse it. Just enjoy being outdoors. If thoughts or worries intrude just acknowledge them and let them go. Just look around, look at the branches on a tree, study a leaf, anything that's about being in the present moment. Essentially, this is meditation. Take long slow deep breaths. Stay there for as long as you wish. If you want to reflect on your thoughts and feelings afterwards, that's up to you. Does this fit in with your idea of what meditation is supposed to be like? Now try other experiences such as a walk in the park, or a walk by the river, or try sitting outside a café just for the sake of being there. Make a note in your diary to meditate in this way at least once a week.

Meditation provides a free and easy way to tune out from the noise of everyday life and take control of your stress response. Its other benefit is that it helps with structural connectivity and slows down the natural ageing process of the brain and protects against cognitive decline. Research indicates that the stress-reducing benefits of regular mediation are cumulative. By association and consequence learning you condition your relaxation response, which provides a buffering effect against stress.

None of the techniques in this book require any special discipline (or philosophy) other than the willingness to try. You could do any of the following exercises out in nature, or in a quiet place at home.

Here's a technique that you can do at the beginning of an extended meditation (and visualization) session, or just on its own to create a sense of balance for you.

Centring (Balancing)

- Sitting comfortably with your back straight and your feet firmly on the floor imagine a small circle around where you sit.
- Take long, slow deep breaths in through the nose and out through the mouth.
- As you inhale, let your awareness/attention fill the circle.
- As you exhale, let your awareness contract to a small point in the centre of your chest.
- Repeat six times.
- Now take a really deep breath, filling the circle of awareness.
- Now exhale, letting your breath sweep through the circle of awareness chasing out any negative feelings and tension.

Just Being a Witness

To help focus and quieten the mind, try this simple technique:

- Close your eyes, induce your relaxation response and picture yourself meditating.

- Throughout the different roles and changing situations and personae in your life, there is an 'I' witnessing it all.
- Ask yourself: 'Who is witnessing this moment?'
- Answer: 'I am.'
- Repeat twice.

Now let's consider a meditation practice that takes into account some of the basic psychological principles we have discussed so far, in particular classical conditioning, as we link, by association, the relaxation response and a trigger phrase (mantra). It's a much more productive and humane use of Pavlov's discovery.

Calmer Mantra Meditation

I use the word 'calmer' like a one-word prayer. Calmer suggests progressive relaxation and it sounds like karma. So try this:

- Sit comfortably in a place where you are not likely to be disturbed.
- Close your eyes and take a long, slow deep breath, in through your nose.
- Hold your breath to the mental count of four.
- As you breathe out through your mouth mentally say 'calmer'. You can say it out loud if you wish.
- If thoughts pop into your head just acknowledge them, let them go and bring your attention back to your breathing and repeat 'calmer'.
- Do this for at least ten breaths.

Maxwell Maltz the originator of **Psycho-Cybernetics**, a forerunner of **Neuro-Linguistic Programming** (NLP) uses the mantra 'calm body, calm mind'. I like to double it to 'calm body, calm mind, calm mind, calm body'. This works well in the next exercise.

Calmer Mantra Meditation (with Muscle Monitoring)

Progressive relaxation of your body is the added ingredient in this exercise. It aims to reduce tension from the tips of your toes to the top of your head. Read the instructions through a few times so that you don't have to rely on the book, then try it out.

- Take three abdominal breaths, mentally (or audibly) saying 'calmer' as you breathe out.
- Then begin to focus on each part of your body, starting with the toes on your left foot.
- As you breathe in, tense your toes.
- Pause for the mental count of four.
- As you breathe out, release the tension and mentally say 'calmer'.
- Repeat this for all parts of your body, working upwards.
- Move up to your calf, then thigh, then move onto the right leg.
- Then, in turn, tense your buttocks, your abdomen, your chest, fingers and hands, arms (each arm in turn), shoulders, neck, face and scalp.
- When you have worked on all of your body, do three more abdominal breaths, repeating 'calmer'.

These exercises condition an association between the word and the relaxed state. Practised regularly and frequently, 'calmer' will acquire the power to interrupt your stress response just by closing your eyes briefly and saying it. In the initial stages, do this meditation two to three times a day (morning, after lunch and evening) for just a few minutes. Do it every day for a month and see how it works for you. Personalize it and try it out with your own relaxing one-word prayer.

Here's a little meditation technique that uses the various of the triangle diagrams in this book.

Confidence Triangle Meditation

Choose a triangle, study if for a few moments, then close your eyes and take long, slow deep breaths to relax. Focus on recreating the triangle in your mind. Let your attention focus on each point in turn, and the going backwards and forwards between the points. Don't try to conjure up associations, just focus on re-creating the image. This helps to implant the learning in your memory.

Just Having More Fun

When you smile you release chemical messengers deep within your brain known as endorphins. Once released, they travel down the spine sending feel-good messages throughout the rest of your body as they go. Endorphins have the effect of pain-killers, reducing physical and emotional pain, as well as providing a general feeling of well-being. This short exercise shows how you can trigger them at will.

Exercise

Research has shown that endorphins are released when we smile and that we can trick the brain into doing this by practising the muscle movements as if we are smiling. When you find yourself smiling, hold a pencil in your mouth between your teeth to force you to maintain a small smile. This muscle movement will trigger endorphins. Do this whenever you feel yourself frowning. Combine it with any of these meditation exercises to compound the effect.

The medicinal effects of laughter are well documented. In fact, a really good laugh has much the same therapeutic effects on the body as deep abdominal breathing. Research has also shown that laughter appears to have a beneficial effect on blood vessels to increase blood flow. We could say that laughter is good for the heart. So, ideally, we should try to find something to laugh about every day, even if it's just watching a comedy DVD instead of a horror film. A daily laugh helps reduce stress, improves respiration (so you gain even more out of your deep breathing), it lowers the stress chemicals and releases 'the pleasure chemical' dopamine. It's often said that laughter is the best medicine. So don't live your life in the placebo group!

Now we've considered the mind, let's turn attention to the body.

Body Wisdom – Let's Get Physical

If physical exercise is your idea of fun then you can also reap the benefits of its stress-busting effects. At the physiological level, regular exercise provides an outlet for the fight-or-flight responses, helping us to burn up stress chemicals. It's also good for us to get away from stress-provoking circumstances for a while and helps distract us from reviewing negative thinking.

Physical exercise can help re-frame our perceptions too. Of course, as we know, exercise has numerous health benefits such as helping to reduce blood pressure, reduce cholesterol, improving cardiovascular fitness, maintaining a healthy weight and improving muscle tone. It also helps release good chemicals in the brain, such as serotonin. This is an important chemical that contributes to a range of functions, including sleep and wake cycles, libido, appetite and mood.

Research has demonstrated that exercise has a positive influence on our mental state, sleep pattern, self-esteem and nutrition. Regular aerobic exercise (such as running, rowing, cycling, swimming and step classes) over a period of a few weeks has been found to reduce anxiety. The greatest benefits are seen in people who begin with lower fitness levels and higher anxiety states. This type of vigorous exercise, several times a week over a period of weeks, is also effective in combating depression, showing the most marked results for people who are heavily depressed. Regular exercise also shows increases in scores of self-esteem irrespective of age or gender. Regular exercise also has a positive effect on sleep and boosts the metabolism, increasing the rate at which food is processed. As if that isn't enough, exercise, especially resistance training (using weights to increase strength not bulk), may help in the formation of new brain cells and boosts cognitive functions including memory. Even a simple walk can help boost attention and memory, and it's even better if you combine it with some breathing and meditation exercises.

Some people live in their heads and divorce themselves from their bodies. Some people use the body to blot out thoughts. It's hard to experience true confidence if you deny a part of yourself. Exercise is a means of reconnecting with your body. At the very least our bodies need a good stretch. We do it every morning but probably not enough to stretch out our muscles and release tension. Practices like yoga and Pilates are excellent for flexibility and core stability, helping to develop the abdominal and back muscles. Following a daily stretching programme, like gym warm-up stretches, has beneficial effects as does having a massage. Remember, if we remove the tension from the body, the brain will complete the process and any mental tension is reduced.

Here are a few simple exercises to experiment with.

Basic Stretching

Stand up straight, close your eyes and stretch by reaching your hands up to the sky and standing on tiptoe. Now return to normal relaxed posture. Repeat this a few times. Then lie on the floor on your back and put your arms above your head and stretch. Breathe deeply while you are doing this and just see how much extra length you can get in your body by stretching a little more after each breath.

Neutral Posture

Stand with feet hip width apart with knees unlocked. Your feet should be slightly turned in, not splayed out. Keep your back straight, neck relaxed and head looking ahead. Relax your elbows, keep your arms a little way from your body, creating a space under your armpits, with your arms, hands and fingers hanging loosely. Focus on your feet making contact with the ground. Feel grounded.

Relaxed Face

- Push your tongue against the roof of your mouth (just behind your teeth) to relax your jaw.
- Lift your eyebrows very slightly, and put a smile in your eyes. Think of how you react to a baby doing something cute and your eyes narrow slightly. Models do the 'smoky eyes thing' to look sexy. It's a cross between a look of quiet benevolence and trapped wind. This will help to relax the eyes and forehead.
- Bring a gentle, almost imperceptible smile to your face.

Now here's an energizing breathing technique combined with physical movement that can help wake you up in the morning and give you an energy boost any time throughout the day.

Pull and Push Breath

- Stand in a relaxed posture and raise your arms above your head in fists (backs of hands outwards, palm side facing you).
- As you breathe in through your nose, pull your fists down to shoulder height, slowly and smoothly, creating resistance as if pulling down on a bar.
- Pause, turn fists (backs of hands now facing you, palm side out), breathe out with an 'aaaah' sound as you begin to open your hands to push upwards, again creating resistance (like

pushing on a bar). Reach up with palms facing the sky and splay fingers.
- Repeat.

These are just a few exercises to help to release tension and create the calm body and a calmer mind. Now let's consider what we put into our bodies.

The Body as a Temple

The computer equivalent of karma is GIGO, an acronym that stands for Garbage In, Garbage Out. When systems break down we often hear the excuse of 'computer error', whereas it's more accurately a programming error. Someone fed the computer a load of old rubbish and, surprise, surprise, a load of old rubbish came out the other end. It's pretty much the same with our bodies. It's called junk food for a reason! It's difficult to feel confident about yourself when you're sweating burger grease. We've already looked at taking control of breathing in order to help you to change your physiology and control your stress cycle. Water, food and exercise are three other things we can control. These will also have an impact on confidence.

Water

Dehydration negatively affects our cognitive abilities, that is the way we process information. Remaining properly hydrated optimizes our information-processing abilities. Drinking water is also good for improving the appearance of the skin. Behave like a prune, feel like a prune and look like a prune. Water is also good for the voice. It helps to keep the vocal folds (cords) moist and so less likely to get hurt when using the voice a lot. Water transports nutrients between cells to regulate body temperature, it dissolves the minerals we need and helps the liver and kidneys flush what we don't need. We pass about one and a half litres of urine each day. We need to keep topping up to match the output.

So are you getting enough water? If you are, good. If you're not, what new hydration goals will you set? If you're still sceptical, why not conduct a personal experiment? Commit to drinking two litres of water each day for two weeks. That's eight 250ml (half-pint) glasses. At the end of that time, review the effects. You have nothing to lose except thirst, fatigue, headaches, wrinkles, muscle cramps and mental confusion. It has to be worth a try. Here are some tips that make it relatively easy to increase your water intake:

- Keep a glass of water at your desk and sip throughout the day.
- Go 'European' and have a glass of water with your coffee (and tea).
- If you find yourself automatically reaching for a cup of tea or coffee, have a glass of water first. It may just be that you're thirsty.
- Have a glass of water with every meal.
- Replace fizzy drinks with a flavoured water (or add a squeeze of fresh lemon or lime to give it a zing).
- Have fresh fruits with a higher water content as snacks.

Food

We've all heard the old adage 'you are what you eat'. Food contains essential vitamins, minerals and other nutrients. Okay, so there are no 'confidence-rich' foods. However, there is plenty of research that demonstrates the links between food and mood. This is beyond the psychological associations there are with different foods. Many people reach for cake, biscuits and snacks to give themselves an emotional boost. A quick-fix slice of cake can cancel out negative emotions. However, more importantly, food can affect our physiology and biochemistry too. Now we all know that there are more diets on the market than there are days in the year. It's not my intention to provide a complete guide to nutrition or offer a 'new-fangled' diet, but just to make a few key points.

Rather than suggesting any of the fad diets, the body of evidence supports the idea of eating a balanced, varied, calorie-controlled diet incorporating the major food groups (proteins, carbohydrates and fats) and cutting down on saturated fats, salt, sugar, processed foods and junk foods. Official government websites provide all you need to know about nutrition and they are based on current evidence. Eating a balanced diet means we are more likely to get the vitamins, minerals, amino acids and other nutrients that have an impact on cognitive functioning and mood.

Case Study: Snack Attack

During part of my coaching training I was seeking volunteers and asked a friend who bluntly replied, 'My life is perfect. I don't need coaching.' He paused then added, 'The only thing I'd want is help with my diet, but what do you know about nutrition?' Now whilst I keep up with the latest developments in research, I am not qualified to dish out advice on diet plans. Instead, I began asking questions. I asked, 'Of all the things you eat, what changes would you make to bring your diet in line with what you think it should be?' Immediately, he said 'I could cut down on snacks, such as potato crisps.' I didn't have to tell him that eleven packets of crisps a day was a few too many. Then I asked how many packets he could comfortably cut down by each day. He decided he could reduce by one a day. I asked when would be the best time to eat his crisps to get maximum satisfaction? He decided it would be as his afternoon snack. Two months later he had lost 7kg (16lb) in weight. The point is that most of us know what foods we are over-indulging in.

Finally a brief thought about controlling our immediate environment.

Mind over Clutter

When we are stressed we become survival-directed and we tend to focus on what we consider to be essential. This may lead us to ignore the impact our environment has upon us. I know when I'm working on a project, my desk tends to become chaotic (well, it does to the 'untrained' eye). I notice that my mind begins to match the clutter and I begin to struggle to focus. What usually helps is to stop what I'm doing and organize the desk. I'll then tidy the room and if I'm feeling really daring I'll get the vacuum cleaner out (if I can find it). Now this creates a much-needed break from mental exertion and provides me with a bit of physical exercise. When I return to my tidier desk and office, I'm more focused and my concentration improves.

Consider this in the context of the *Confidence-Karma Chain*. I took action to change the environment, which had the knock-on effect of changing my feelings and re-energizing my thoughts and actions. So consider what you can do to create a more pleasant environment and how this will affect your relaxation levels and your ability to focus. We might extend this approach throughout our homes by generally de-cluttering and donating unwanted things to charity. That way you make a difference in your own life and other people benefit too.

So there you have it: there are numerous ways in which you can control stress in your life. Some of the techniques require very little additional time investment. None of them cost anything either. So consider what you will commit to over the next month to try out as personal experiments and assess the impact on your confidence and esteem.

Review: Finding Your Keys

Review the *Confidence-Karma Chain* in Chapter 1 to see how the things we have considered in this chapter relate to other aspects of confidence building. This chapter has focused on the link in the chain to do with environment, other people and situations, as well as skills and the mind–body connection and ways of taking control of stress, and increasing relaxation. The ability to relax is offered as the foundation for all confidence building. Now consider the important review questions:

- How do you rate your confidence at the conclusion of this chapter?
- What's better for you in terms of confidence?
- What have been the most effective aspects of this chapter in taking you forward?
- What knock-on effects do you imagine there will be if you put the information in this chapter into practice?
- What will you put into practice?

Karma Call

Consider how these new insights can help you to build confidence in others. Write down three affirmative actions you will take to continue the process. What are your *Confidence-Karma* goals after reading this chapter? 'In order to see changes, what changes will you be?'

1.

2.

3.

In the next chapter we consider techniques for managing impressions, including communication skills and body language. We also consider ways of developing assertiveness.

Chapter 4

All The World's a Stage ...
Impression Management

Act the part and you will become the part.

William James, 1842–1910, psychologist and philosopher

Preview

Building on the mind–body insights from the previous section, Chapter 4 offers practical tips and exercises for creating positive first impressions and improving communication skills, including by awareness of body language, and by developing assertiveness.

Making the Small Stuff Count

We don't build confidence using complicated, convoluted techniques or acts of recklessness. We begin with the small stuff, the everyday things we often take for granted. Developing the themes introduced earlier, this chapter presents interrelated sections with accompanying exercises designed to get you (or the people you are helping) to practise the small stuff. It's basically a crash course in impression management through a series of exercises you should treat like personal experiments. The emphasis is again on taking action and assessing the results. Try them on for size and write up the results in your journal.

What Makes a Good First Impression?

We form impressions of other people very quickly. Research has shown that we make survival-related decisions ('Is this person a threat?'), in laboratory conditions, in under two seconds. It can, however, be as fast as 30 milliseconds. We form a virtually instantaneous impression of whether we find a face attractive or not, but we usually wait to speak to the person before making a decision. I'm sure you can all think of celebrities who appear very attractive until they open their mouths. Before we continue, let's conduct a little (non-scientific) experiment.

Consider two people:

Person A: Intelligent, skilful, industrious, tense, determined, practical and cautious

Person B: Intelligent, skilful, industrious, relaxed, determined, practical and cautious

Now consider the following list of words:

Which of the following do you think also apply to Person A (circle as many as apply)?

Generous, humorous, sociable, popular, reliable, persistent, serious, restrained, strong, honest

Which of the following do you think also apply to Person B (circle as many as apply)?

Generous, humorous, sociable, popular, reliable, persistent, serious, restrained, strong, honest

---

Did you see Person A as serious and restrained and person B as generous, humorous, sociable and popular? You probably rated both of them as reliable, strong and honest.

. So which person would you prefer to work with, or spend long amounts of time with? Which person would you like in your team? Who do you think you'd like the most?

The Halo Effect

This experiment is based on psychological research in the 1940s by Solomon Asch. In psychology we know that impressions of others are often formed around a central trait that creates a halo effect. In Asch's experiment he presented people with a list of adjectives describing a fictitious person. One group had the list: intelligent, skilful, industrious, warm, determined, practical and cautious. A second group had the same list but with 'cold' replacing 'warm'. Both groups were presented with a second list of 18 trait words (different from the original list) and were asked to underline those that best described the target person. The 'warm' group chose generous, popular, humorous and sociable, while the cold group choose the opposite traits. In a subsequent experiment, another psychologist, George Kelley, also found that a group of students reacted more favourably to a teacher when he had been labelled 'warm' as opposed to a teacher who was labelled 'cold'. Further research got similar results using different pairs of words.

So what does this tell us?

- Some words just seem to go together, such as humorous, popular and sociable.
- We like to see people in a consistent way and it's quicker and simpler to group similar traits together. This is another side-effect of cognitive economy. We can't process every bit of information that comes our way, so we make a few short cuts. In effect, we play the odds and take an educated guess.

In the above experiment, I replaced the words 'warm' and 'cold' with 'relaxed' and 'tense'. If you want to make a good first impression, never underestimate the power of appearing relaxed (including a smile) to create a halo for other positive traits. So if you haven't been practising the relaxation exercises in Chapter 3, take this as further encouragement.

Body Language Broad Strokes

When trying to create a good first impression the temptation is to become an avid reader of body language books. The problem is that much that is written about body language is based on generalizations, a lot of speculation (and some outright fantasy). Even the most famous statistic about body language, the ubiquitous 55% – 38% – 7% rule is widely misinterpreted. The rule is often stated, incorrectly, that in *any* communication the words we speak only account for 7% of the total message. Tone of voice accounts for 38% and the largest proportion, 55%, is down to non-verbal communication, that is what we commonly call body language. This was not the conclusion of the original research. The findings only applied to forming first impressions and situations where there was a conflict between verbal and non-verbal communication. They did not apply to *every* communication. Furthermore, the experiments were carried out in laboratory conditions so they might not translate exactly into the real world. We simply cannot control the extraneous distracting variables in the real world as we can in the lab. Added to this, the people who took part in the original experiments might not have been representative of the general population. There also might have been cultural biases and limitations. So, although the research offers a useful general principle, it is important to interpret the findings with caution and not get too carried away.

You only have to be aware of the main 'broad strokes' of non-verbal communication, given that impressions are formed rather quickly. Not surprisingly, the most important things you can do are relax, be honest and be yourself. If you are relaxed, communication becomes more natural. If you are honest you don't have to worry about concealing deceit. If you are yourself you don't have to worry about keeping up a pretence. With these three simple principles in mind, all else should fall into place.

Six Broad Strokes for Confident Communication

1. Relaxation is key (and is covered in the previous chapter)!
2. Posture
3. Facial expression
4. Gestures
5. Personal space
6. Voice and speech

Posture

A useful acronym is **SOLER**, which stands for:

- Squarely face the other person
- Open posture
- Lean towards the other
- Eye contact
- Relaxed (so important it appears again and again)

We lean our bodies towards things that interest us and do it naturally when relaxed. We lean back to distance ourselves from something. We angle our bodies away from a person as a way of indicating we want to leave or that something else (more important) is demanding our attention. Adopting an open posture signals that we have nothing to hide. People often employ the palms-open gesture to signify openness. However, it's also important to be cautious in our interpretation. People may be folding their arms because they are defensive, because they are cold or simply because it's more comfortable. In body language analysis it is usually important to look for clusters of behaviour. However, this is also where discrepancies and differences of opinion arise. Just be aware that most people are looking for open posture.

Watching stand-up comedians, I'm always put off by the ones who deliver their jokes with their eyes fixed on the ceiling. I keep looking up to see what they are looking at and miss the jokes. Much has been written about eye contact and how to get the balance right between looking at the other person and breaking eye contact to look away. In formal situations or first encounters, lack of eye contact may be interpreted as shiftiness, untrustworthiness, shyness, nervousness, feeling intimidated or a lack of confidence, or a host of other reasons. So if you have an issue with eye contact, it makes good sense to address it. Making good eye contact cuts down on all the guess work the other person has to do. You may have observed that as people get closer and more comfortable, they tend to break eye contact more often. An often-quoted estimate is that we should make eye contact for two thirds of the time and glance away for the remainder. One technique is to look at the other person's left eye for a third of the time, then the right for a third and then away for a third. I mentioned this technique to a friend. He followed it with such precision that he looked like the psychotic doll, Chucky, from *Child's Play*. We both fell about laughing. These general rules provide rough indicators but followed too rigidly they suppress what we do naturally when we are relaxed.

Exercise

Consider in which situations you are more comfortable making eye contact. Do the kind of situational analysis that we did in Chapter 2 with confidence levels. What conditions, including people, make for the best eye contact for you? How do you do this? Have a bit of fun and try the rule of thirds for eye contact with a friend or colleague. Firstly, exaggerate and make it very obvious. Then make it more subtle until you find the level that feels comfortable for you and the other person.

Facial Expression

In coaching (and counselling) training, the main emphasis is on matching the facial expression with the words and feelings. We don't expect people to say 'that's interesting' and then roll their eyes in contempt. It's about being genuine. If you relax and listen (rather than drift off with your own thoughts), it becomes automatic. There will be more on listening skills later in the chapter.

Exercise

Have fun experimenting with a friend. Mismatch facial expressions and then take a few deep breaths, relax, listen and react. Get feedback from each other as to whether the facial expressions were appropriate.

Gestures

Again, if you are calm, honest and yourself the gestures should take care of themselves. We all have idiosyncratic gestures. We don't all have to become clones. It's just about becoming aware of any nervous fidgeting or distracting behaviour. Appropriate hand gestures tend to emphasize keywords whereas inappropriate ones tend to confuse the message. The best way to see your own trademark gestures is to watch a film of yourself or get feedback from a friend.

Personal Space

Space invaders are those people who stand closer than relationship dictates. Generally, the closer we are to someone emotionally the closer we can stand physically. With strangers we usually approach them at arm's length and keep a distance of about one metre. As we get to know a person we allow them closer. Judge how well you know a person and observe how they position themselves in relation to you. If they back off, you're too close.

Voice and Speech

When nervous we speak more quickly and lose fluency. Just slowing things down a little can help a lot. People with esteem or confidence issues may also speak more quickly, assuming that others will only listen to them for a limited time. People with confidence are not afraid to leave spaces. You don't have to become a great orator and you don't have to abandon your regional dialect and acquire a fake telephone voice. Speaking more slowly and avoiding jargon and region-specific phrases is usually enough.

Exercise

Conduct your own exercise by going to a coffee shop to observe how others interact. Keep it relaxed and casual. Other people are not supposed to know you are observing them. Just decide whether the interaction is relaxed, formal or informal. Note who looks comfortable and confident. It's not wise to eavesdrop, so just focus on non-verbal communication. Are the people using SOLER? What else do you observe?

Exercise

Over the next few days practise SOLER on people around you, such as family, colleagues and friends. What do you notice about their reactions? How does it feel for you?

Finding Your Voice

Breathing, sleep and hydration all have an impact on our voices. If we don't get enough of each of these, our voices suffer. Here are a few exercises that can help in projecting the voice.

Warm-up

Just pick a pitch that's comfortable for your voice. To get the mouth, lips and tongue warmed up, say all of the vowel sounds out loud. Make each one short and distinct, exaggerating the mouth movements. Next, make each vowel sound blend into the next. Then repeat the short, distinct vowels. Run through the consonant sounds (buh, cuh, duh, fuh, guh, and so on), making them distinct and again exaggerating the mouth movements.

Sing

If you need to give a speech or presentation, sing as a preparation. A good choice of song is 'Do-Re-Mi' from *The Sound of Music*. It's an upbeat sound and it uses all of the notes in the scale. Just have fun with it, but don't strain the voice.

Bean Bag Projection Technique

This is a technique to improve voice projection. For this exercise you need one of those small beanbags you used to have at school, or a ball is fine too but not if you are in small room. Standing up in neutral position, take a few deep breaths, look across the room, fix your gaze at a point and throw the bean bag towards it, at the same time firmly saying 'yes' or 'no'. This is a good exercise to practise when you are walking a dog. You can take a ball and practise projecting your voice with this technique every time you throw the ball and say 'fetch'.

Building Rapport

The six broad strokes to confident communication will also build rapport with other people. There are two additional techniques taught in coaching and counselling training: **mirroring** and **matching**. These techniques can be difficult to use subtly and can appear obvious, contrived or clumsy. Also, if you focus on relaxation and listening, then mirroring and matching happen spontaneously.

Mirroring

When we are in rapport with another person, our non-verbal communication may become similar and mimic each other in subtle ways, so occasionally it looks like a mirror reflection. However, mirroring is quite subtle and doesn't happen consciously. Forcing it can appear manipulative and actually damage an encounter if the other person notices.

Matching

This is perhaps the more useful of the two techniques and usually occurs when we are actively listening to another person. We match their language and use some of the same words as they use. To see how this works you only have to notice how a group of close friends often express themselves in similar ways.

Playing with Status

Theatrical improvization games often explore the notion of the status of characters as it is important to convey this quickly to an audience. It's probably an over-simplification, but as a general rule people are perceived as having higher status if their voice and movements are smoother and measured rather than erratic. It is interesting to play around with this in everyday life especially with situations that you may find intimidating, such as returning a faulty item to a shop. Standing up straight, making eye contact, speaking clearly and slightly more slowly, keeping gestures and facial expressions to a minimum, will convey a much better impression than gibbering away with your head flailing around like a bladder on a stick.

> ### Exercise
>
> Pair up with a friend and role-play status interactions. You can have fun with this by having a low status competition. This doesn't mean immediately throwing yourself to the floor and muttering 'I'm a reptile and I eat mud.' Instead try making very subtle adjustments so that it remains believable. When you've practised this, find your receipts and take those unwanted items back to the shop.

Listening Skills

Rarely in everyday life do we get undivided attention from another person. When we do, it can be a powerful experience. This is one of the core features in a therapeutic relationship such as counselling. It's also key in coaching too. Listening is a key skill of the *Confidence-Karma Approach*. When people are listened to, they feel validated. If you feel nervous talking in social situations, don't underestimate the value of being a good listener. Let's begin with listening barriers.

Barriers to Good Listening

It's difficult to listen to someone else when you are preoccupied by your own thoughts and problems or panicking about what to say next. Maybe you have no interest at all in what this person has to say or maybe you don't like them. You may be struggling to keep up as they are speaking too quickly or using too much jargon. It may be a noisy environment or you are too hot or too cold. It may be that you are late for an appointment or simply hungry or thirsty. Any one of these factors (or a combination of them) can have a significant impact on our ability to listen. Practising mindfulness exercises can help you to increase general awareness.

Active Listening

Active listening is more than just being a 'sounding board'. It's important to signal to the other person that you are listening. This helps to move the conversation (monologue) along. Here are a few signposts to good listening:

- Show you are attending with nods and affirmative noises.
- We often don't speak in perfectly formed sentences so listen until the other person indicates by a gesture or expression that they are ready for your response.
- Reflect the other person's feelings, such as saying 'that sounds terrible' when they have told you about 'something terrible'. This simply indicates that you have gauged the emotional tone of the conversation. If the other person is laughing you should at least be smiling.
- If you don't understand something then ask for clarification (you could say, 'run that by me again').
- If appropriate ask for an example.
- Use open questions rather than closed questions (who, what, how, where, when).

Questions, Questions and More Questions

Television interviewers like to tell tales of their most difficult interview. The interviewee is described as uncooperative, difficult or 'having a bad day'. However, when we get to see the actual interview, we notice that the interviewee only 'grunted' yes or no, because the interviewer's questions were mostly closed, only requiring one-word answers. Invariably the questions were predictable, routine or downright inane. It would be like having an audience with the Dalai Lama and asking him 'Is orange your favourite colour?' It's hardly likely to uncover the meaning of life. I've also seen nervous interviewers fire off three or four questions, leaving the interviewee bewildered and wondering which question to answer first, assuming they can remember them all. Here is a brief guide to question types:

- **Open questions** are the 'who', 'what', 'how,' 'when' and 'where' questions. This category usually includes 'why' questions. However, 'why' questions are often best avoided as they can sound like you're conducting an interrogation. Replace these with a simple 'How come?'

Examples of open questions are: What is your favourite colour? How could things be different? What's the next action you are going to take in confidence building? When would be the best time to try this out? Where would be the best place to try out this new behaviour? Who will be the person to notice that you're behaving more confidently? How do you like to spend your time? What do you think of the weather?

- **Closed questions** limit the options for response. You've probably seen television courtroom dramas where the witnesses are told 'Just answer yes or no.' The intention is to force a response. They are all-or-nothing type questions that don't encourage disclosure.

Examples are: 'Do you feel confident?' The open version would be 'How confident do you feel?' Or try 'Is that accurate?' and compare this with 'How accurate is that?'

- **Leading questions** are usually thinly veiled statements with a token closed question tagged on, such as 'The weather is really rubbish today, isn't it?' The open version would be 'What do you think of the weather?' or 'How is the weather suiting you?' I know someone who often asks questions such as 'Don't you think you were a fool to change jobs?' The implication is 'you are a fool'. A better approach would be 'How is the change of job working out for you?'

- **Multiple questions** can be open, closed or leading questions or any combination. For example: Did you try out the confidence building exercise? (closed). How was it? (open). Did you get a lot from it? (closed). I bet you feel a lot better now, don't you? (leading). Clearly there is too much to process and if you throw in a 'why' question it begins to sound like an inquisition.

So use open-ended questions one at a time and let the person answer. Use closed questions sparingly when you just need to clarify a point. For example 'So what you are saying is . . . [paraphrase] . . . Is that right?' If you relax it's easier to avoid multiple questions.

Exercise

Try practising questions with a friend taking it in turns to be the questioner. Pick a topic such as a holiday and begin by asking just closed questions. Then switch to asking open questions. Now reverse roles and try it again. Discuss how the two different question types feel both for the person asking and the one answering. Now find opportunities to try out open questions in social situations.

Self-Disclosure

Self-disclosure is the process of revealing your inner self to another person. It helps with acceptance as people form positive impressions of people who give something of themselves. Getting the balance right is important. Rushing up to strangers in the library and offering to show them your appendix scar and confessing your darkest secrets is hardly likely to win you friends, although it may influence people to avoid you. So when is enough, enough?

Self-Disclosure Quiz

Here's a short quiz to explore self-disclosure issues. Rate each of these statements on a scale from 0 to 10, where 0 equals 'have never mentioned to anyone' and 10 equals 'I have disclosed everything about this to everyone I've met.' This includes status updates on social networking sites.

0	1	2	3	4	5	6	7	8	9	10
No		Low			Moderate			High		Very high

1. ___ General worries (money, health, wealth).
2. ___ What really gets on your nerves.
3. ___ Things that make you happy and bring joy to your life.
4. ___ Areas of yourself you'd like to improve (fitness, health, confidence, skills).
5. ___ Dreams, goals and ambitions.
6. ___ Sexual activity and love life, including graphic details.
7. ___ Your weaknesses and negative character traits.
8. ___ Hobbies and interests.
9. ___ What makes you angry and what happens when you are.
10. ___ Things in your life you are ashamed of or feel guilty about.

Scoring

This quiz is intended as a discussion point and not a scientific assessment. The cut-off points only provide general feedback. If your score is close to the edge of a range, then also look at the other band too.

Zero speaks for itself. You are a closed book, inside a pad-locked buried chest, with a prison built on top of it.

1–20 indicates a closed person who doesn't like to give much away. Sharing something with others provides an opportunity for feedback. Focus on less personal areas and make small disclosures. Hobbies and goals are a good place to start.

21–60 indicates a moderate level of self-disclosure. Just be aware of higher scores and don't be over familiar with unfamiliar people. Scores towards the middle of the band indicate a balance between your private self and public openness. If you score is below 30, also read the feedback for the lower band.

61–81 indicates an open person with high levels of self-disclosure. Some of these topics may make others uncomfortable or cause them to judge you harshly or take advantage of you. Openness is often a good thing provided the other person can handle it, wants to handle it and you can trust them. Spare a thought for the feelings of your listeners.

90–100 indicates that you are very open. In fact there isn't much you won't disclose and are happy to do so with anyone who will listen including people who'd prefer not to receive so much information. Beware of becoming like the celebrity reality TV stars who live their lives like an open wound. Focus on the more neutral areas for disclosure and include the personal stuff more sparingly and with fewer people. Some things are better kept to ourselves, and one or two trusted friends. Beware that your self-disclosure doesn't become habitual dumping on other people for free therapy.

Safe for Disclosure?

A simple way to consider where you might be self-disclosing too much or too little is to rate each of the above ten topics on a safety scale. How safe for general, detailed disclosure is each topic, where 10 equals 'totally safe' and 0 equals 'Shhh! Don't tell a soul'.

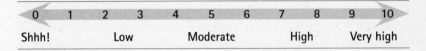

| 0 | 1 | 2 | 3 | 4 | 5 | 6 | 7 | 8 | 9 | 10 |

Shhh!   Low   Moderate   High   Very high

If these scores match roughly with your first set of scores, your disclosure level for this topic is about right. However, if there is a gap between the two sets of scores then you need to make adjustments. For instance, if you rate sexual activity as a 5 for safety but a 10 for disclosure, maybe it's time to keep a few details to yourself.

Small Talk

Some people complain that small talk is pointless and superficial, but it's more likely that they just don't know the ground rules, the topics to pick and those to avoid. You may worry that you're being too banal and the other person will think you a bore. Here are some general pointers to build on what we have already covered in this chapter:

- Use SOLER and smile.
- Introduce yourself, tell them your name and ask theirs, then use their name occasionally. Don't wear it out and tag it on to every sentence like sales people on commission like to do.
- Use open questions to draw the other person out.
- Keep it light and focus on the positive. Talking about the weather is fairly neutral but don't launch into a rant about how it depresses you.

Here are some examples of topics that attract people and topics that will have them running for the hills.

Subject Matter – No Dark Materials

Likely to attract: saying where you are from, a recent film or TV programme you liked, saying what you do and where you go to relax, pets, recreation interests, books you've read, your name, food, the weather, clothes, holidays, places to visit, theatre productions, concerts and commenting on something in the immediate environment.

Add your own examples of neutral topics, things you might talk about just to pass a pleasant afternoon. No, it's not meant to be racy and exciting! It's okay to pick subjects on which you might disagree, but best to avoid those that might lead to an argument.

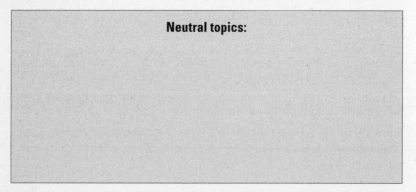

Neutral topics:

Likely to repel: talking about ailments, sex dreams, religion, being a know-it-all, discussing your sex life or asking questions about theirs, talking about infidelity or swinging, asking someone's salary, asking whether people own their own home, racism, political correctness, politics, paedophilia, capital punishment, abortion, vivisection, animal rights, pornography, discussing bodily fluids or body parts that have gone septic or the power of prayer as a tool against evil.

What other topics are better avoided if the aim is to spend a pleasant afternoon over scones, jam and clotted cream, sandwiches with the crusts cut off, and a pot of Earl Grey tea?

Topics to avoid:

Exercise

Practise your small-talk skills with a friend as a fun exercise. Start by keeping it light then have your friend try to steer the conversation to darker matters. You should try to steer it back to the lighter side of life. Then swap roles. Once, you have had a few practice runs and a few laughs, go out and try it on someone you don't know, at the bus stop or in a supermarket queue. However, this time just keep it light. No mischief!

Moving the Conversation On

The most common opening questions are:

- What do you do for a living?
- Where are you from?

Neither of these questions is going to set the world of conversation alight. Instead of asking a question about work, I ask 'How do you like to spend your time?' This is more likely to get a positive response as people don't necessarily enjoy their jobs or want to talk about work. They might be between jobs. Offer them the chance to talk about things they enjoy, which might include their job. If you do get stuck with the 'work' question, you could state your job and add 'and it funds my hobby or passion'. Then you get to talk about something you enjoy. With a bit of extra information or self-disclosure, you can open up the conversation and move it on.

People worry about what to say once the opening questions have been asked. A good strategy is to research your place of birth, where you live and somewhere you'd like to live. A fun or interesting fact about a place can help the conversation along. For instance, when asked where I am from, I could answer that I'm from Birmingham but live in the Black Country, birthplace of the Industrial Revolution and award-winning actress Julie Walters. Or I could add that I split my time between Birmingham and Edinburgh but I dream of living in Greece. Doing this provides more routes for the conversation to take. However, beware of going off on a monologue and hogging the conversation. Don't speak for more than 60 seconds. It's more than long enough. The simplest way to get the conversation back to the other person is to tag on 'and how about you?' Then exercise your listening skills. Don't be too eager to jump back in with your own story. It's not all about you.

Exercise

Research your home town, where you live, and where you'd like to live and find out a few fun facts about each. Practise an opening conversation with a friend or colleague. Just have fun with it. What other small-talk questions are you commonly asked? Use these principles to consider options for your answers.

What's Going On

Keeping up to date with what's going on in the world has never been so easy. There are 24-hour news channels on TV and news feeds on the internet, television debate shows and of course the humble newspaper. You don't necessarily have to invest massive amounts of time and become a media expert. Just set aside a little time each day to find out what's happening in the world. Never be afraid to admit you don't know what's going on. That's your opportunity to ask questions. Many people love to offer their opinions, which means you get an opportunity to practise your listening skills. Afterwards, check out the news story and get your angle on it and form your own opinion. There's bound to be another opportunity to chat about it.

Exercise

Seizing an opportunity to visit an elderly relative or check up on elderly neighbour is a simple way of giving something to other people and practising small talk skills. Chatting to other neighbours, a shopkeeper or the person delivering the post are other useful opportunities. What others can you think of?

How Assertive Are You?

Non-assertive people let things happen to them without saying anything or making their feelings known. Some people may even describe themselves as 'doormats'. They know it's happening, don't particularly like it, but often feel powerless to do anything about it, except 'beat themselves up'. So what's the alternative? Well, for many people the difficulty lies in working out the difference between assertive and aggressive, especially as the words are often used interchangeably. There's a fine line between the two. Remember John from the Introduction who didn't want to take part in my warm-up exercises? He probably thought he was being assertive but he came across as quite aggressive. His reaction was probably what we might expect when dealing with inappropriate body contact from the office lecher. It was not what we might expect from being warmly invited to take part in a fun, ice-breaking exercise.

Assertiveness Quiz

On a scale of 0–10 rate the following statements, where 0 equals 'totally disagree, not at all like me' and 10 equals 'totally agree, exactly like me'. You are free to use any point on the scale.

1. ___ I say no without apology if people make unreasonable demands of me.
2. ___ I express my opinions, even if others disagree with me.
3. ___ I find it easy to ask friends for small favours.
4. ___ I prefer to 'nip' problems in the bud rather than let them escalate.
5. ___ When I think a person is being unfair I draw his/her attention to it.

For the remaining questions, the scale is reversed: 0 equals 'totally agree, exactly like me' and 10 equals 'totally disagree, not at all like me.

6. ___ I often feel intimidated by opinionated people.
7. ___ I often end up saying 'yes' when I really want to say 'no'.
8. ___ I show my anger by swearing at people or belittling them if I think they need it.
9. ___ I sulk or give people 'the silent treatment' to make a point or get my own way.
10. ___ I tend to let others walk over me and treat me like a doormat.

Total: ___

Scoring

As a general guide, as the items in the quiz are self-explanatory:

- 0–40   indicates low assertiveness.
- 41–60   indicates moderate assertiveness.
- 61–100 indicates high assertiveness.

If you have a low score on question 8 it indicates a tendency for aggressive behaviour.

Aggression is not an extension of assertiveness. It's a mask. Assertiveness is firm and up-front but calm, relaxed, open and honest. Assertiveness is about believing that everyone has a right to express themselves honestly and make their feelings known. Aggression values none of this. Aggression is overbearing, threatening, demanding and often belittling. Aggression is about pushing for what you want with very little regard for the wants, needs and feelings of other people. If we measure confidence by relaxation and creating an environment where others flourish, only true assertiveness meets those criteria. Being assertive doesn't necessarily mean that you always get your own way. It means being able to speak up and put your case and yet recognize the right of others to hold different opinions. Aggressive behaviour gives rise to a culture of aggression, bullying and a lack of respect. Assertiveness builds a culture of respect where people feel comfortable speaking their minds and encourage other people to speak theirs.

Exercise

Review the scores for individual questions for your areas of non-assertiveness and pick one to work on. Imagine what has got you to this score and not a lower score. Concentrating on examples of past assertiveness, however small, offers you something to build on. Now imagine what you would be doing at the next point along the scale. Set yourself a small assertiveness goal and take action on it.

In the following section, there are suggestions for helping other people become more assertive. You may also want to try some of these out for yourself.

Personal Experiments in Assertiveness

Throughout *Unlock Your Confidence* there are repeated calls to build confidence in continuous, small but significant steps, assessing the feedback as you go, and building on it. This includes seizing small opportunities to pass on confidence to others. Here are some personal experiments.

Set Goals

The most important thing you can do to overcome shyness and build assertiveness and confidence is to start with very clear ideas of which behaviours you want to change. Think of everyday situations where it would be useful to be more assertive. The exercises in Chapter 2 helped you to identify areas for improvement. It doesn't necessarily have to be something you rated at a low level; it could be a strength that you want to develop further.

Conversations with Strangers

One of the easiest ways to develop social skills, become more assertive and develop confidence is to strike up conversations. You can begin practising with friends before transferring these skills to the relative safety of the supermarket. If Hollywood films are to be believed, there's a lot of flirting done over the fruit and vegetables. If this seems too bold, then simply ask an assistant or another shopper for directions to a particular aisle. Ask people for their opinions of products. If you see someone taking something off the shelf that you haven't tried before then ask them about it. Queueing offers another opportunity to strike up conversations.

A while ago I realized that I've been passing the same shop a few times a week for about a year and not once have I said 'good morning' to the shopkeeper, who usually stands in his doorway. So I set myself the small goal of greeting him each time I passed. I now stop for the occasional chat and a laugh. So are there any people you pass by whom you could smile at and say good morning to?

Practise SOLER

Shyness is often interpreted as being uninterested. Using SOLER skills can counter this impression. If you take an interest in other people, they will reciprocate.

Telephone Calls

Are there opportunities for you to make a telephone enquiry? We've become so used to communicating by text or email that we don't exercise our voices as much any more . Try contacting your utility companies by phone, even if it's just to give a meter reading. Make a call to your mobile phone provider just to see if you can get a better deal. If you're going to visit a tourist attraction, call beforehand to find out the opening hours, especially if the weather's bad. Maybe there are friends and family whom you could call more often, especially ageing relatives who may really value the sound of a friendly voice.

When I decided I fancied doing some radio work, I started by calling in to a local radio talk show to voice my opinion. It wasn't long before they started calling me. I went on to have a long-running spot on the show. The first time I called my old stutter came out. After about a dozen times, I was able to relax more, and so more of the real me came across. Seek out your own opportunities to connect on the telephone. Having a stutter wasn't a reason NOT to try, it was the reason TO try.

Practise Saying 'No' to Street Canvassers

It's become a fact of life that you can't walk down the street without someone leaping out at you trying to sell you something or asking if you've had an accident. A popular way to deal with these situations is just to ignore the person and walk straight past. However, this misses an opportunity to practise assertiveness skills. It's also important to remember that these are real people often just trying to do a job. You don't have to buy into what they are selling but you can seize the opportunity to behave assertively (and respectfully). My approach is to make eye contact and say politely but firmly 'Sorry, I don't conduct business in the street.' You need to work out your own official line and just stick to it. If they try to ask you questions or engage you in a conversation just repeat your official line, bid them goodbye and then walk on. This approach can work in other situations. It's what I call the broken android technique. If someone is pressuring you, know your position, state it firmly and then stick to it, repeating it until they get the message.

Enrol in a Class

The easiest way to widen the circle of your friends and seize opportunities for small talk is to join groups or clubs with similar interests. If you're a member of a gym, try out a range of classes. Learning new things is a good for building confidence, esteem and assertiveness. Classes and groups offer opportunities to ask questions, seek opinions and offer your own. They offer opportunities to chat before and after, and may also lead to other social opportunities.

Haggle

Visit a car-boot sale and haggle over prices. Ask if that's the best price. Half the price and then ask 'How close can you get to that?'

Remember it's only a bit of fun so don't take it to heart. Similarly don't get carried away and come home with a load of old tat. Of course, you may also want to try selling stuff at a car-boot sale to become experienced in being on the receiving end of the haggling.

What other things can you think of, and what will you try?

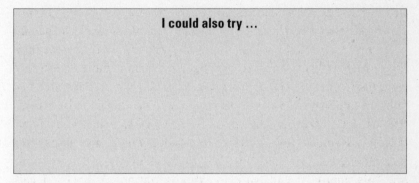

I could also try ...

The Give and Take of Feedback

A free and open exchange of opinions and perspectives inevitably means dealing with feedback that can feel anything but constructive. It also includes the simpler social conventions of giving and receiving compliments and praise. Sometimes the people who complain of never receiving compliments or praise are also less likely to give them out. As Mahatma Gandhi said, 'Be the change in the world that you want to see in the world.' Someone has to break the pattern. This section builds on all of the skills we have covered and experimented with in this chapter.

The Gifts of Compliments and Praise

The ability to accept praise and compliments graciously is not usually thought of as a skill. Many people feel uncomfortable doing so. Consider your own reactions to compliments or praise. Do you:

1. Argue with the person and demand they take it back?
2. Argue for the contrary evidence, listing your faults and failings?
3. Laugh in embarrassment and say 'It was nothing'?
4. Ignore the praise/compliment altogether?
5. Look embarrassed, grunt or mumble an acknowledgement, but do not make eye contact?
6. Say thanks, hurriedly or sharply, and quickly move the conversation on?
7. Make eye contact and accept graciously (smile and say thank you)?

Which option most closely matches your reaction? If you answered any of responses 1–6, instead consider that it wasn't a compliment or praise, but that someone gave you a gift. Now I'm guessing you wouldn't snatch it out of their hand and throw it in the bin saying 'Well that's a load of old crap.' So how has your answer changed?

It's socially appropriate to accept graciously. You don't have to believe the compliment. However, just by acknowledging positive experiences you can change your perception of yourself. Difficulty in accepting compliments and praise is not always about confidence and esteem. It could just as easily be a lack of practice. If you were raised in a household where compliments were rare, then you don't gain the experience of accepting them.

Before looking at the spirit in which to accept compliments, let's consider why people offer them. Basically it's about reciprocal liking ('I like you because you like me'). If you say something nice then people will think you are a nice person and are more likely to be nice in return. Compliments build rapport and are also good conversation starters. It doesn't always work but that's the guiding principle. I remember my first advice to someone to use a compliment. A school friend really fancied this girl and didn't know how to approach her. I suggested that he casually pay her a compliment. I think our definitions of casual were very different. He waited for her to come out of the toilets and then leapt out, made her jump, and blurted out 'I like your frock!' I suppose, given the circumstances, it could have been worse, Needless to say, that love remained unrequited.

If you are giving a compliment, most importantly of all, make sure it's genuine. Keep it simple and keep it small, if it's just an ice-breaking type compliment. It's better to say to someone 'I like your brooch' rather than some over-blown, phoney and quite transparent attempt to ingratiate yourself. People will accept small compliments more readily than grand cringe-worthy displays. The aim is to give someone a little uplift, not embarrass the hell out of them. Don't follow one compliment after another, 'and I like your hair, and I like your bag, and I like your shoes', and so on. Yes, we get the message, you like lots of things. It sounds obvious but people often fall into this trap when trying to impress someone. If you are attracted to someone or want them to like you, the stakes are higher, stress levels increase and perspective goes out of the window.

Think of praise as a combination of a compliment plus re-inforcement to repeat the behaviour. If you thank someone for doing a good job, they are more likely to repeat it.

Exercise

Praise yourself in the mirror at the end of a good day or as you have successes. Look yourself in the eye and say 'Well done,' or 'You did well today.' If you cringe it's a sure sign that you need more practice doing it (and accepting compliments in general). Continue doing it until it doesn't make you cringe. Afterwards, continue doing it anyway.

Giving and Receiving Feedback

Often it's also not what we say but how we say it. Editing and framing what we want to say determines whether or not other people will listen to us and actually hear what we have to say. So here are some general pointers that can be applied to most situations:

- **Too much, too soon. Feedback overload.** Be aware that material with a high emotional content will take longer to process. We have to deal with the feelings before we can get to the thoughts. You don't have to deal with emotive topics all in one go. So, if you're raising a number of issues, start with the most important, stay calm and keep it brief. It's also okay for the person on the receiving end to ask for 'time out' to process it. Trying to cover everything in one session inevitably means that at least one of you will 'think out loud' and may regret it. The conversation then goes off at a tangent. If you get into the habit of communicating on a regular basis, openly and assertively, there isn't that imperative to have to deal with everything in one go.

- **Think partner rather than adversary.** Assume you both have a 50:50 stake in a win–win situation. It doesn't have to be a zero-sum game. Make an effort to listen and see things from the other's perspective. Better still, accept 51% of the responsibility for reaching that win–win situation.

- **Pick the right moment.** Don't be tempted to dive in, no matter the time or place. Agree on a time and place that works for both of you to discuss important matters when you are not likely to be disturbed or distracted. You both need to feel safe to disclose your intimate thoughts.

- **Own your statements.** When dealing with negative or difficult issues you need to own your statements. There is a big difference between the ownership of 'I feel' and the blame of 'You make me feel.' Once you've said 'You really make me sick', there isn't really anything else left to say. If you introduce a sense of blame, the whole discussion gets sidetracked. Do you want to talk about blame or do you want to take about the actual issue?

- **The behaviour is not the person.** It is far easier for a person to change their behaviour than to change their whole self. Be specific.

- **Factual observations not judgements.** Don't introduce your spin on what things mean, such as 'If you were a decent human being . . .' or 'If you were professional . . .' These are not facts: they are your perceptions. Introducing subjects such as decency and what it means to be professional are philosophical discussions. Do you want to talk about philosophy? If not, stick to what you have actually observed and let this lead the conversation.

- **Give specific feedback based on observations.** Words like 'always', 'sometimes', 'often' and 'never' are all vague. This introduces too much scope for disagreement. Put things into context and be more specific. It can be easy to get side-tracked by arguing over the terms and frequencies rather than discussing the real issues.

- **Share ideas or offer alternatives.** Most people respond better if they have a sense of input or investment in a course of action, so asking questions is usually more productive than making demands or giving advice. Nobody likes being told what to do. Discussing options should be the first step in any 'negotiation'. You could even use a SWOT analysis. Psychologically, there will be a greater sense of ownership of an idea for both people if they have both contributed to it and feel that their input has been valued.

- **Ask questions to open up negative feedback.** Instead of
  shunning and avoiding criticism it sometimes helps to get
  further information. So if someone tells you that you did
  something poorly, ask them 'What was poor about it?' Poor
  is very vague and subjective. If you solicit more information
  you find out what 'poor' means to them. Continue with
  'what', 'where', 'who' and 'how' questions. This will allow you
  to understand why the other person thought you performed
  poorly. It doesn't necessarily mean that you agree with all
  that they say. Ultimately you can say 'I understand why you
  thought my performance was poor.' They feel listened to and
  you may have some useful feedback.

Something Else for the One-Minute Promo

More thoughts, feelings, attitudes and values:

Review: Finding Your Keys

Review the *Confidence-Karma Chain* in Chapter 1 to see how the
things we have considered in this chapter relate to other aspects
of confidence building. This chapter focused on the effects of
new behaviours in creating good impressions and improving
communications. Review your experiences and then answer these
questions:

- How do you rate your confidence at the conclusion of this chapter?
- What's better for you in terms of confidence?
- What have been the most effective aspects of this chapter in taking you forward?
- What knock-on effects do you imagine there will be from putting the information in this chapter into practice?

Karma Call

How do these new insights help you to build confidence in others? Write down three affirmative actions you will take to continue the process. What will you pass on to other people in your life? 'In order to see changes, what changes will you be?'

1.

2.

3.

In the next chapter, we explore the role of attitudes and values in shaping our view of the world.

Chapter 5

Attitudes, Values and Meaning

If you want to enlarge your life, you must first enlarge your thought of it and of yourself.

Orison Swett Marden, 1850–1924, writer

Preview

In this chapter we consider the role of attitudes and values in shaping your view of yourself and structuring your world. It considers how our view of human nature influences our self-image and how the way we view the world influences what we do in the world, and vice versa. It develops ideas around auto-prejudice and introduces a programme for improving our attitudes towards ourselves.

What Are Attitudes and Values?

Attitudes exert a dynamic influence upon the way we respond to the world. We all have them and express them in the words we use and the choices we make. They are a key element in our psychological make-up. As discussed in the Introduction, they create a mental state of readiness to act, or react, to objects, situations and people. Psychologist William James argues that to change our attitudes is to change our lives. This is a key principle of confidence building.

Values are beliefs on which we choose to structure our lives. They represent what we consider to be good, desirable, worthwhile and valuable, psychologically and morally. Values provide a sense of what we ought to do and motivate us to act to support those values. Attitudes provide a structure and values provide the standards which guide our action. Whenever we use the put-down 'Don't judge me by your standards,' we are conveying our values. Attitudes shape the way we make sense of the world and values act as our internal GPS (Goals Positioning System). We may hold hundreds of attitudes but considerably fewer values. Genuine confidence is based on a true understanding of our inner values and attitudes and an appraisal of our skills and strengths. When we know where we stand in life and what we stand for, we can build confidence from the inside out.

Reviewing the *Confidence-Karma Chain*, you'll notice that attitudes and values occupy the central position. This puts them in the strongest place to influence both ends of the chain and shows how crucial they are in confidence building. This chapter invites you to explore your attitudes and values and offers an auto-prejudice reduction programme. Let's begin with the function of attitudes and how they structure our world.

How We Use Attitudes

Attitudes filter our experience and help us make sense of the world, allowing us to determine what we need to pay attention to and what we can ignore. According to psychologist Elliot Katz attitudes serve four main functions for us:

- **Instrumental function:** Attitudes at the most basic level are our likes and dislikes. They are the simple evaluations of good/bad, positive/negative, useful/useless. We are drawn to things that benefit us and repelled by things that disadvantage us. Attitudes help us to maximize gains and minimize losses. This role of attitudes explains how some people choose political parties, based on the 'What's in it for me?' principle. We are more likely to change our attitudes if doing so helps us to fulfil our goals or avoid negative outcomes. So how does the label of 'confident' versus 'unconfident' impact on our likes and dislikes?

- **Knowledge function:** Attitudes help us to organize our perceptions quickly and impose a meaningful structure on the world. They help us to evaluate how new stuff fits in with what we already know and to maintain order and stability in our personal frame of reference. The downside is that we have a tendency to work with broad generalizations, in the form of stereotypes. Sometimes we jump to premature, erroneous conclusions. Our attitudes change when we alter our frame of reference, or when evidence overwhelmingly contradicts our attitudes (pre-judgement). As you work through this book and consider new information or reappraise old ideas, how does it affect your conclusion about yourself regarding confidence levels (auto-prejudice)?
- **Values expression function:** Attitudes express our value system and reinforce our self-image, our sense of who we are and what we stand for. We cultivate attitudes that we believe indicate our core values. Consider what attitudes you might cultivate to demonstrate your core values. What behaviours follow on from these?
- **Ego defensive function:** Attitudes may help to protect us from acknowledging basic truths about ourselves or the harsh realities of life. They serve as defence mechanisms. For example, people with feelings of low self-esteem and low confidence may develop an attitude of superiority, 'over-confidence' or aggression to compensate. We consider defence mechanisms in greater detail in the next chapter.

According to Katz, attitude change is achieved not so much by changing a person's information or perception about an object, but rather by changing the person's underlying motivational needs, that is their values. We'll explore values later in the chapter. In the meantime, let's consider the manifestation of negative attitudes that create a block to confidence building.

Auto-Prejudice

I introduced the concept of auto-prejudice at the beginning of the book as a core theme in the *Confidence-Karma Approach*. Preparing for this chapter, I reviewed a number of definitions of prejudice and first I'd like you to consider how you'd feel about someone who subjected you to any of these:

pre-judgement	pre-conceived opinion	faulty generalization
unreasonable attitudes	unfavourable opinions	negative attitudes
unreasonable suspicion	hostility	fear
antipathy	hatred	bias

Taken together they don't leave any space for you to be you. So, from these words, let's define auto-prejudice as 'pre-conceived, unfavourable and unreasonable attitudes based on faulty generalizations directed towards the self'. To put it another way it's 'having a downer on yourself without considering all of the facts'. Prejudice is simply the tendency to pre-judge based on insufficient or inaccurate information.

This book is essentially one big exercise in challenging your ideas about confidence and how they apply to you. It works on the assumption that how you view the world affects what you do in the world and vice versa. This includes our view of ourselves (self-image) and our abilities (efficacy). Here's another triangle to illustrate the link:

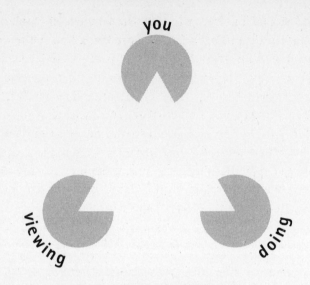

The You–Viewing–Doing Triangle

Auto-prejudice contains internalized and often distorted negative appraisals we have received over the years from family, teachers, bosses and the media. It often operates automatically, below our conscious awareness, rather like a bad habit. Auto-prejudice contains feelings and thoughts and often hostile actions, such as putting ourselves down and avoiding opportunities to challenge our negative attitudes. So if we look at the *Confidence-Karma Chain*, we tackle auto-prejudice by working on behaviours, thoughts and feelings (as we are doing throughout the book) to control our negative attitudes. We work with skills and strengths (as we did in Chapter 2) to influence our attitudes and explore our values, which also has a knock-on effect towards both ends of the chain.

Looking at prejudice more generally in social psychology, we can find two main theories explaining its origins. Theodore Adorno and colleagues published *The Authoritarian Personality* in 1950 to attempt to explain the atrocities of the Second World

War. One strand in this work was the concept of intolerance of ambiguity. In short, the tendency to use black-and-white thinking makes us uncomfortable when we can't neatly classify something. Some people are intolerant of ambiguity and uncertainty to a greater degree than are others. The other key work is Milton Rokeach's *The Open and Closed Mind*. Two aspects of this are lack of flexibility and closed-mindedness leading to a rigid outlook on life. A characteristic of both of these theories is black-and-white thinking and rejecting anything that occupies the grey area. We considered black-and-white thinking in Chapter 2 (strengths) and we explore it in more depth in Chapter 7 (resilience).

Exercise

Consider what persistent negative attitudes about yourself hold you back? What attitudes contribute to a 'can't do' mindset? Consult a close friend or someone you trust to get another perspective. What would they say are your self-defeating put downs? Pick one negative attitude to challenge, write it down at the top of a page and then list all of the evidence to the contrary.

Muddying the Waters

Imagine you've been labelled as having 'low confidence' by other people and you don't agree. You decide enough is enough and you're going to do something about it. You're going to have a 'low confidence rebellion' and set about stirring things up and 'muddying the waters'.

- What attitudes, feelings, thoughts and actions would challenge the low confidence label?
- What would you stop doing and what would you start doing instead?

- What would you be doing for someone else to notice that you are more confident and the old label doesn't apply?
- If you are free from the expectations of the low or no confidence label, what else would you be doing, feeling and thinking?

One way in which attitudes shape our view of the world is in our ideas of what it means to be human.

Assumptions about Human Nature

Social psychologist Lawrence Wrightsman has conducted extensive research into attitudes about human nature and has highlighted several factors by which we judge the social world. Other commentators on his research have argued that the 'self-accepting' person tends to view the world as a friendlier place than does the self-rejecting person. So consider the following items and circle your responses:

- **Agree or disagree?** Most people are basically honest and trustworthy.
- **Agree or disagree?** Most people are basically altruistic and try to help others.
- **Agree or disagree?** Most people have a lot of control over their lives.
- **Agree or disagree?** Most people have a good idea of their strengths and weaknesses.
- **Agree or disagree?** Most people will speak out for what they believe in.
- **Agree or disagree?** You can't accurately describe a person in a few words.
- **Agree or disagree?** People's reactions differ from situation to situation.

Do your responses make for a safe and friendly world or an unsafe and hostile one? How do these attitudes shape your social interactions, especially in relation to confidence building? Which of these attitudes are most likely to act as an obstruction to your personal development? Explore exceptions to this attitude and reconsider this obstruction. The bottom-line question is: do these attitudes express your values and maximize positive opportunities for you? How do these attitudes affect your self-image, self-esteem and self-efficacy? Do they support your long-term goals?

Case Study: The Luxury of Learning

I coached a final year student (Alistair) for motivation for exam revision. At the end of the session I asked him for feedback. The thing that made the most impact for him was attitude change. He had complained that he couldn't 'get into' revision as there were too many distractions and he was more interested in going out socializing. In short he resented having to study and miss out on all the fun. We tend to learn more effectively when we approach learning in a positive frame of mind. Otherwise we are fighting to retain information that we are, at best, indifferent towards. I asked him, instead of seeing learning as getting in the way of life's luxuries, what if he saw this learning opportunity as a luxury? Of course, for many people it is a once in a lifetime opportunity.

We discussed how he might change his learning environment to be more comfortable and even make it fun. Context plays an important part in how we learn. If we study in a familiar, relaxed environment this context becomes associated with the learning and provides cues for recall.

Alistair left the coaching sessions, changed his attitude about learning, enjoyed the luxury of study and ended up with a very respectable grade in his final exams. Consider Alistair's example and how the changes he made fit into the *Confidence-Karma Chain*. Ultimately, I appealed to his value system to decide what was more important to him: a few nights out with friends or a good education.

Confidence Karma Auto-Prejudice Reduction Plan

I have reviewed prejudice reduction plans in social psychology and compiled an unprejudiced plan based on the material in this book. This acts as mid-point revision, and also provides a summary of things that you can encourage others to do to challenge their auto-prejudice. Some of the things have been covered in earlier chapters and some are coming up later in the book. Which items on the list could form the basis for your next confidence-building goals?

- **Build confidence in others** – this can be as simple as making more of an effort to compliment, praise, express gratitude and listen to others. Spend time listening to other people. This could be at home, with your extended family, friends or at work (*Karma Calls*).
- **Communicate clearly** – adopting a communication style that is clear and unambiguous is part of being assertive. Don't drop hints or sulk and expect people to be mind-readers (*Chapter 4*).
- **Positively stated goals** – to support your strengths and values and build confidence (*Chapters 7 and 9*).
- **Look after your health** – this includes making time for relaxation, exercise, drinking water and eating a varied diet. It's more difficult to feel good about yourself and pass on positivity if you are dehydrated, have heartburn and no energy. A piece of cake may give you an instant high but a little exercise can trigger the release of feel-good chemicals and boost your metabolism. People who are ill look inwards not outwards (*Chapters 3 and 6*).
- **Do your bit to save the planet** – don't be put off with doom and gloom arguments that it makes no difference. Do something anyway (*Chapters 6, 7 and 9*).

- **Join a social group and share a common interest** – making friends with like-minded people can boost self-esteem and develop and maintain social skills and communication skills (*Chapters 4 and 6*).
- **Find opportunities to laugh and have fun** – it's difficult to have a downer on yourself when you're laughing (*Chapter 3*).
- **Take a course on absolutely anything** – it doesn't really matter what you learn. Don't be put off by people who say 'It's a waste of money,' or 'You'll never make any money doing that.' Do not underestimate the knock-on effects of learning something new (*Chapter 2*).
- **Travel** – again it doesn't really matter where. Getting out of your routine is the important thing. A change of scenery can bring about a change in perspective. You may find yourself doing things that you wouldn't normally do, which make you re-evaluate who you are and what you can do. Experiencing different customs and values may cause you to reappraise your own (*Chapters 2 and 6*).
- **Broaden and build** – focus on investing time in positive emotions to create a buffering effect for stress and a broader pool of possible responses in stressful situations (*Chapters 3 and 7*).

Update for the One-Minute Promo

Thoughts, feelings and attitudes:

We Are What We Value

Values are our inner motivators. They underpin the choices we make. Values are quite simply what we 'stand for' in life. They are the things that give life meaning and purpose. Social psychologist Milton Rokeach argues that there are two main types of values that guide us. **Terminal values** are ultimate destination values. They represent the final point in our journey (terminus). He makes explicit the connection between values and goals and refers to these values as **desired end-states**. These include kinship (unity), peace (of mind), equality, justice, wisdom, happiness or just having an exciting and fulfilled life, and so on. The other type are **instrumental values**; these represent a desirable means to achieve our desired end-states. We use these to help us to get to where we want to go. These desirable attributes include helpfulness, ambition, competence, being hard-working and so on. Instrumental values are closely related to our strengths. Positive Psychologists Martin Seligman and Christopher Peterson describe strengths as 'values in action'. So at this point review your list of strengths from Chapter 2.

Our values work as an intricate system. Even friends who share the same values may find themselves in disagreement on a major news story. It's the way we combine our values, what we prioritize and how they interact with one another, that gives us our unique take on the world. This means that, sometimes, we may hold conflicting values that work against each other such as 'freedom' and 'security'. Tough decisions often reveal our values hierarchy. Ultimately some things are more important to us than others and we may need to compromise one of our values in favour of another. Within our system of values we do not necessarily always represent them as positive end-states we want to move towards (**approach values**). We sometimes express them in terms of what we want to move away from (**avoidance values**). So as well as representing what we stand for, they also represent what we stand against. So people who stand against injustice and discrimination are embracing the values of justice and inclusion.

Answer these questions from your own perspective, then from the perspective of a close friend or loved one, and finally from the view of an objective observer.

- Knowing yourself as you do, what do you stand for in life?
- What inner (psychological) qualities push you forward?
- What are your ultimate goals in life, your desired end-states?
- On which values in life are you most likely to clash with others?
- Thinking of a value system you strongly oppose, what values do you hold instead?
- What values would you be prepared to die for?
- In your obituary or on your gravestone, what values would you most want to be remembered for?
- If you could wave a magic wand, what values (end-states) would you bring to the world?
- Which of your values support confidence and esteem in yourself and others?
- What values are currently informing your life choices?
- Knowing yourself as you do, what values do you sometimes overlook or dismiss?
- Anything else?

Don't be in a rush to hurry through the questions. Ask the 'anything else' question a few times. Sometimes we need that extra prompt and extra thinking time to dig deeper. Have you included self-confidence and self-efficacy as instrumental values (something to get you closer to your ultimate goals)? What about self-esteem as a preferred end-state? If you included these, what would you do to demonstrate them? What actions, thoughts and feelings communicate 'self-esteem'?

From the above questions, compile a list of your values, making a note of which values are ultimate end-states and which are instrumental in getting you there.

Exercise

Select the ten ultimate (end-state) values most important to you. Write each value on a separate slip of paper. Now place them in order. This is your values hierarchy (which may fluctuate from time to time). Select the top three values and decide what immediate actions you can take to support them. Repeat this exercise every week. Consider what you will do to remind yourself of your values throughout the week.

Walking the Walk and Talking the Talk

Consider your goals and everyday life and ask whether you are taking action in line with your desired end states, your values? Consider this rating scale and supplementary questions and write the answers in your journal.

Upholding Your Values

Rate the extent to which you are currently upholding your values, where 0 equals not at all and 10 equals totally.

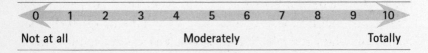

0	1	2	3	4	5	6	7	8	9	10
Not at all					Moderately					Totally

- How have you got this far along the scale?
- What is it that has helped you to get from 0 to where you are now?
- What do you imagine doing when you are one point up the scale that you aren't doing now?

- What small, significant action will you take to support your values over the next week to further your personal development?
- What opportunity, however small, will you seize over the next week to uphold your values and support your personal growth?
- Once your actions are focused on upholding your values, what effect do you imagine it will have on your self-confidence and self-esteem?

Good Enough?

As you did for your strengths evaluation, consider what would be 'good enough' for you in terms of a values/behaviour match. Take time to consider these questions thoroughly and write the answers in your journal.

- What will represent 'good enough' for you? What number on the scale?
- How will you know when you get there? What will you be doing differently to what you're doing now?

Case Study: Different Path, Same Destination

I worked with Niall who was applying to prestigious business schools to do an MBA degree. There were numerous questions on the form that he was struggling with. After the first session, we established that all the questions were variations on the themes of goals and values and how to match goals and values. At the start of the sessions Niall had a very clear direction he intended to take and part of this was informed by family expectation. As he explored his values, he began to realize that there was more than one path he could take to meet his values. One of his core values was 'making a contribution' and 'giving something back'. After four sessions, he decided not to pursue the MBA at that time. Instead, he applied for a promotion at work that better suited his strengths. He also set up a small business to put his values into practice immediately. He then set the MBA as a longer-term goal. Again, consider how Niall's story fits into the *Confidence-Karma Chain.*

Necessary and Sufficient Conditions for Change

For therapist Carl Rogers the most important factor in successful therapy is the therapeutic relationship guided by three interrelated values (put into action). In lay terms these are: **sincerity, acceptance** and **understanding.** According to Rogers, these attitudes help clients to express themselves freely without feeling that they are being judged. Rogers's term for acceptance is **unconditional positive regard.** This is closer to Dryden's argument (Chapter 1) that acceptance should be our aim rather than esteem, that is positive regard with conditions attached. So these are offered as core values in your approach to helping others build confidence.

Rogers stated that we always move in a positive direction when the 'necessary and sufficient conditions' are met (including those above). Matching goals to values is a crucial condition for getting us primed and ready for action to chart the course of our lives. Mahatma Gandhi argued that our values are our destiny. By matching your goals to your values you programme your motivational SatNav. This brings with it a sense of confidence that you are moving in the right direction.

Something Else for the One-Minute Promo

Thoughts, feelings, attitudes and values:

Review: Finding Your Keys

Review the *Confidence-Karma Chain* in Chapter 1 to see how the things we have considered in this chapter relate to other aspects of confidence building. This chapter has focused on the values and attitudes link in the chain. Consider these review questions and write the answers in your journal.

- How do you rate your confidence at the conclusion of this chapter?
- What's better for you in terms of confidence?
- What have been the most effective aspects of this chapter in taking you forward?
- What knock-on effects do you imagine there will be if you put the information in this chapter into practice?

Karma Call

How do these new insights help you to build confidence in others. Write down three affirmative actions you will take to continue the process. What will you pass on to other people in your life? 'In order to see changes, what changes will you be?'

1.

2.

3.

In the next chapter, we explore needs, perspectives and defence mechanisms and how they impact on confidence building.

Chapter 6

Needs, Perspectives and Defences

From without, no wonderful effect is wrought within ourselves, unless some interior, responding wonder meets it.

Herman Melville, 1819–1891, novelist, essayist and poet

Preview

In this chapter we consider a number of psychological principles distilled from psychotherapy with the aim of getting you to think about, in greater depth, your feelings, actions and thoughts from different perspectives. We also consider how all this impacts on confidence building.

A Sense of Perspective

Many psychological concepts have filtered through into everyday language. Often we use them without recognizing their origin, such as 'ego'. In this chapter I ask you to consider a number of concepts from psychology and psychotherapy. The aim is use these to consider how the insights impact on confidence building rather then to engage in an in-depth analysis of the theories. A key part of unlocking confidence is about getting a better insight into what makes you tick, that is what pushes you forward and what holds you back. So we'll consider motivation and how we defend ourselves against unpleasant thoughts and feelings. The chapter looks at a range of defence mechanisms and how they might distort your self-image if you hold on to them too long.

All of the various theories are offered as different lenses through which you can view your feelings, actions and thoughts.

The ideas expressed in this chapter are not meant to be in-depth analyses of psychological theories. Instead, I ask you to consider some familiar concepts to see how they relate to confidence building. The emphasis is on creating a slightly different perspective, and suggesting different lenses through which you can view your feelings, actions and thoughts. The chapter explains different defence mechanisms which distort the self-image.

Survival and Self-Actualization

Psychologist Abraham Maslow offers a hierarchy, or pecking order, of human needs arguing that we are subject to two basic motivational forces: **survival** and **self-actualization** (growth). This hierarchy is expressed as a pyramid, with basic needs at the base and the higher need of self-actualization (realizing our true potential) right at the top. You can see how this ties in with the broaden and build ideas in Chapter 3.

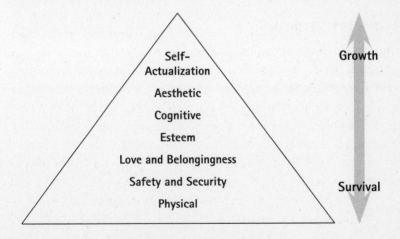

Maslow's Hierarchy of Needs

Survival includes physical and psychological factors such as meeting basic physiological needs and attaining safety, defined as a sense of belonging, love and esteem. So, for Maslow, self-esteem and self-efficacy are essential for survival. However, esteem needs are half-way up our hierarchy of needs and if we are not meeting the needs below, self-esteem is harder to achieve. Let's consider the levels in the hierarchy.

- **Physical needs** (at the base of the hierarchy) include our requirement for food, drink, sleep and rest, exercise and activity, regulation of temperature, bodily elimination and sex (not necessarily in that order).
- **Safety and security needs** (at the next level up) include protection from danger, including that posed by physical illness. Threats can be both physical and psychological, so this may also include the need for routine and familiarity to counter a fear of the unknown.
- **Love and belongingness needs** include how we benefit by being part of a group, and psychological needs such as trust and acceptance, and giving and receiving love and affection.
- **Esteem needs** include self-esteem and self-efficacy, the respect and esteem of others and the ability to give it.
- **Cognitive needs** including the need for meaning in life.
- **Aesthetic needs** include the appreciation of beauty in nature and art.
- **Self–actualization** is the need to reach one's potential.

Maslow's theory emphasizes that lower needs must be satisfied before we can attend fully to the next level up, although I'm sure you can think of exceptions such as the tortured artist who is able to create in abject poverty. The higher up the hierarchy the greater the need is linked to life experience (in a psychological sense) and less to a biological imperative. Also, as we ascend, it becomes more difficult to meet the needs. As with many human goals, they are only met through a series of steps. *Confidence Karma* acknowledges the importance of lower needs in building confidence and esteem. That's why Chapter 3 is on mindfulness and general health and why the Introduction attempts to meet safety needs by revealing the structure from the start. The whole approach encourages belongingness by working with others and emphasizing the value of passing on confidence to others.

Exercise

Review the material we have covered so far and relate it to the hierarchy of needs. Consider which of the lower needs you are not currently meeting, such as physical needs, safety needs and belongingness needs. What small step could you take along the path to meet these needs? Also consider, in what ways does the *Confidence-Karma Approach* address needs of meaning and beauty? How does it encourage you to realize your potential? What would you do differently if all of your esteem needs were being met? What other insights do you have when considering the hierarchy of needs?

Self-Actualization Statements

These statements represent key attitudes and behaviours that lead to self-actualization. There is no score for this exercise, unless you choose to apply one. It's enough to consider which ones are like you and which are not like you. Tick the ones that apply and put a cross by those that don't.

____ I can tolerate uncertainty in life.
____ I accept myself for what I am.
____ I accept others for what they are.
____ I value spontaneity in life.
____ I focus on solutions.
____ I have a good sense of humour and like to have fun.

___ I am able to look at life objectively.

___ I express my creativity.

___ I can express myself and resist pressure to conform to the crowd.

___ I show concern and take action on human rights and the well-being of the planet.

___ I appreciate, deeply, basic life experiences.

___ I have established deep satisfying relationships with a few people.

___ I have peak experiences in my life.

___ I appreciate life with childlike wonder.

___ I appreciate life with full absorption and concentration.

___ I enjoy trying new things instead of sticking to safe paths.

___ I am able to listen to my own feelings in evaluating experiences.

___ I don't feel like I have to follow tradition for tradition's sake.

___ I take responsibility for my life and work hard.

___ I have identified my defences and have the courage to give them up.

Write out the two separate lists in your journal. If you identify with a statement, what can you do to demonstrate this further in your life? If you don't identify with a statement, what might you try out as an experiment so that you would identify with it more?

If you have already adopted all of these attitudes and values to some degree, which ones will you select now and set some small positive goals and take action on them? Also, consider which parts of *Confidence Karma* encourage actions to satisfy the items on the list. If you wish to score the above items, use the 0–10 scale, where 0 equals 'totally not like me' and 10 equals 'totally like me'. Your total score will range between 0 and 200. To convert this to an overall 0–10 scale, divide the total by 20.

The final item on the self-actualization list refers to defence mechanisms, so if you haven't already ticked that item, the next section offers you an opportunity to do so.

Defence Mechanisms

Defence mechanisms are the psychological tricks that we have evolved to protect ourselves against, and avoid dealing with, unpleasant emotions and realizations. Defence mechanisms are unconscious strategies to deal with uncomfortable realities that are a threat to our sense of self. In effect they are ways in which we deceive ourselves to deflect from a truth too painful to process. They may be useful in the short term to deal with immediate threats, but not as a long-term strategy for building inner confidence and improving self-esteem. Scan down the descriptions below to spot if you are using any of these defence mechanisms to block change.

Instead of taking action, we sometimes alter our perceptions. We may kid ourselves that we can work around it or muddle through, Classic statements like, 'If people don't like me the way I am then it's their problem,' are about defending against change. Confidence building is about recognizing our habitual and ultimately self-defeating defence strategies and finding the courage to give them up. Just tick the items if you recognize them as strategies you have used.

____   **Acting out** is performing an (often) extreme behaviour to express thoughts or feelings without full awareness of the emotion that drives the behaviour. An example of this is self-harm. The physical pain is an expression of what one cannot bear to feel emotionally. Another is risk-taking bravado as a substitute for inner confidence and self-esteem.

____   **Fantasy** is the attempt to solve psychological conflicts by retreating from the real world. An example would be spending large amounts of time on computer games to gain a sense of achievement.

____ **Passive aggression** is the tendency to behave aggressively towards others in an indirect way, such as painting oneself as a victim and engaging in emotional blackmail. An example is blaming other people for one's own procrastination.

____ **Projection** is when we attribute our own unwanted thoughts, feelings, beliefs, motivations and behaviours to others. The object of projection invokes in that person precisely the thoughts, feelings or behaviours projected. For example, gossips always complain about other gossips, the gossips then gossip about each other. 'I hate you,' becomes 'You hate me.'

____ **Somatization** is when we turn in on ourselves and transform negative feelings towards others into pain, illness, anxiety and self-harm.

____ **Hypochondria** is a preoccupation and excessive worrying about having serious illness or a series of ailments (often in alphabetical order). Being ill can bring attention and significance, and also acts as a reason for inaction.

____ **Intellectualization** is about focus on the intellectual aspects of a situation to the exclusion of the emotional aspects. It's about creating an aura of aloofness or reading a self-help book and evaluating the ideas in it but doing nothing about them. Yes, I had to sneak in another call to action.

____ **Rationalization** is about making excuses or putting things into a different light, for instance not winning a competition and then concluding that it was a rubbish competition in the first place. Offering a different explanation for one's perceptions or behaviours in the face of changing circumstances.

___ **Reaction formation** is about taking the opposite view to one that causes anxiety. Putting on a brave face, or being polite to people you can't stand and even going out of your way to be nice to them. Effectively this is denying your true feelings, which has a negative effect on self-esteem.

___ **Regression** is about dealing with negative impulses and emotions by behaving like a child. Taking to your bed, or eating when upset or depressed, or having a temper tantrum, or sulking are some examples.

___ **Repression** is about blocking out threatening (but pleasurable or desirable instincts), often in the case of sexual impulses.

___ **Withdrawal** is a more severe form of defence. It entails removing oneself from events, stimuli, interactions, etc. under the fear of being reminded of painful thoughts and feelings. Retreating into one's own world.

___ **Displacement** is about choosing a substitute object for the expression of your feelings because you can't express them openly to the true target. For example, arguing with your partner because you're angry with your boss. Again it's about being true to your own feelings.

Exercise

Consider how defence mechanisms impact on confidence building. Are there any defence mechanisms that you identify with? Which ones would have a positive impact if you let them go? Write down some examples of when you used the defence mechanisms. With these new insights, and the benefit of hindsight, what alternatives could you consider next time a similar situation arises?

Now let's consider some alternative positive defence mechanisms that help us to deal with conflicting emotions and thoughts whilst enhancing a sense of control, enhancing pleasure in life and optimizing positive outcomes in life and relationships. Many of these concepts are integrated in the *Confidence-Karma Approach*. Tick the ones that you recognize as your strategies.

____ **Altruism** provides the pleasure and satisfaction we get from helping others. In terms of confidence we also enjoy the beneficial effects of passing it on (*see Introduction*).

____ **Anticipation** is about planning ahead and predicting future obstacles, threats and discomfort. This is where the SWOT analysis is useful (*see Chapter 2*). It involves realistic planning to avoid future discomfort.

____ **Humour** can give pleasure to yourself and others. It is also a way of diffusing situations and dealing with challenging aspects of life. People faced with a disaster sometimes say 'Well, you just have to laugh, don't you?' Self-deprecation in small doses is an indication that people don't take themselves too seriously (*Chapters 3 and 4*).

____ **Identification** is the process of modelling oneself on another, including their values, character traits and behaviour. It is often done at an unconscious level. In confidence building we do this consciously and strategically (*Chapter 5*).

____ **Sublimation** is about transforming negative emotions or instincts into positive actions, behaviour, or emotions. For instance, stress becomes excitement. Sexual tension can be channelled into exercise (*Chapters 2 and 3*).

____ **Compensation** is the process of emphasizing strengths to counterbalance perceived weaknesses. Recognizing that we cannot all be strong at everything and focusing on strengths helps to build esteem and support a positive self-image (*Chapter 2*).

___   **Assertiveness** is about speaking up for ourselves, expressing
our opinions and needs in a firm, respectful manner. It
is also about listening when we are being spoken to. It is
undeniably one of most helpful defence mechanism and a
key feature of desirable communication skills (*Chapter 4*).

Exercise

With which of these productive, positive defence mechanisms do you
most identify? Which of these could replace those you identified from
the previous list? What would be the impact on confidence, self-esteem,
self-efficacy and self-image? Take time to review earlier chapters and
read sections again. You may also wish to re-try exercises or try the
ones you missed first time around. Pick three of the positive defence
mechanisms and take an action to put each into practice.

Beyond Analysis

Psychoanalyst Sigmund Freud has perhaps contributed more than
anyone else to the understanding of the human condition, both
in terms of other therapists who built on his work and those who
railed against it. For our purposes we will consider some basic
principles to create different perspectives with which to view confidence building. Freud is associated with the three concepts that
comprise the personality, Id, Ego, Superego (although the words
Freud originally used are 'The It', 'The I' and the 'Above I' [or
'Over I']). Let's consider these in turn.

The **Id** (or the It) is the part of our personality that is directed
by the **pleasure principle**. It is primitive, disorganized and self-
centred. It's all about instant gratification of our basic drives. It
works very much to the 'I want it and I want it now' principle. It
seeks to avoid pain, including the 'pain' of waiting. Id impulses
bubble away, often below the surface of conscious awareness.

Newborn babies could be described as 'little, bouncing bundles of Id'.

The **Superego** (the Above I) is the internalized sense of parents, parental figures and society standards. It's a kind of conscience.

The **Ego** (the I) works to the **reality principle** and is stuck in the middle trying to pacify the needs of the Id and the Superego. The Ego works to a sense of occasion and cultural norms.

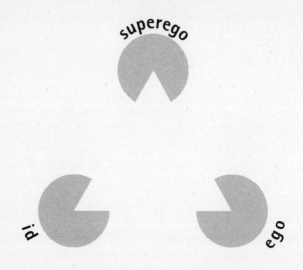

Freud's Personality Triangle

Let's consider the Id, Ego and Superego as three perspectives on life, goals and confidence building. Are you rather impetuous and live in the moment without a care for social convention or appropriate behaviour like the Id? Are you paralysed by 'oughts' and 'shoulds', quite traditional and worried about transgressing societal norms like the Superego? Or are you the realist who looks for the right avenues to balance the opposing pull of the Id and Superego?

It's true that the term 'ego' has become a bit of a dirty word for some. We use 'ego' to refer to an inflated sense of self, big-headedness. So let's be clear what ego means in the *Confidence-Karma Approach*. Taking the three letters, EGO can stand for environment, goals and outcomes.

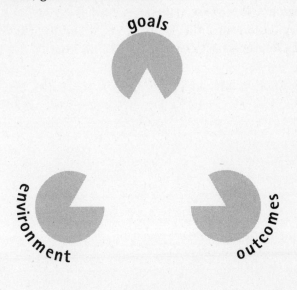

The EGO Triangle

Our goals, environment and outcomes are all inter-related. The EGO seeks the optimal match. I came up with this definition after trying to create a diagram for change to support the *Confidence-Karma Chain*. I wanted to account for environmental and situational variables, feelings, thoughts, actions, goals and outcomes. Once I isolated the EGO components, I was left with the attitude triangle of **feelings**, **actions** and **thoughts**, that is, the means to balance E G and O.

This represents a simplification of Freud's work (and a bit of poetic licence) but it is enough for us to consider the impact of these personal structures on confidence building. They show how we can be torn by different and competing needs. If the Id has a free reign you'll probably end up getting arrested. If the Superego exerts too much control over you then your personal development will be arrested. The Ego may help you work out a different approach that helps you meet your goals and live to your values without getting arrested in either sense of the word. Do you recognize situations in which delaying gratification might be more advantageous? Do you bind yourself with 'shoulds' and 'oughts' to the point where you do nothing at all? Or, do you work to the reality principle by considering environmental conditions, decide what outcomes you want and then create achievable and realistic action plans for your goals to achieve them?

Growing Up, the Inner Child and Parental Guidance

Another therapeutic approach, influenced by Freud, is also amenable to the triangle approach. This is **transactional analysis** developed by Eric Berne.

We don't need to delve very deeply to see that its model of development has something to say about how we develop and maintain confidence. TA argues that we have three main (ego) states we interact with and use to make sense of the world: **Parent**, **Adult** and **Child**.

In the **Parent** state we feel, act and think in ways that mimic our parents, or how we interpret our parents' actions. (This includes actions of other parental or authority figures.) There are two sides to this state. There's the **nurturing parent** and there is the **critical, controlling parent**. Some parents, in a misguided attempt to protect their children from hurt, end up trampling on their children's dreams ('It'll only end in tears'). Hearing the parental words 'But why didn't you do it this way?' is not a recipe for improved performance, it's the language of 'Nothing you do is ever good enough, so why bother?' Other parents tell their children they can achieve no matter how unrealistic this may be. Yet other parents support and encourage their children in the child's individual strengths and skills. The parent state has parallels with the superego.

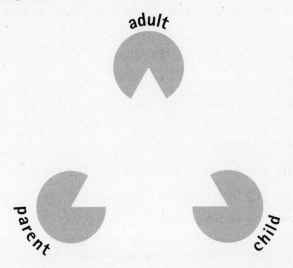

The Transactional Analysis Ego States Triangle

Take a moment to consider the parental messages you have internalized and write the answers to these questions in your journal.

- How do you feel, act and think based on your parental view of the world (or your perception of it)?
- How does your parent state affect your confidence?
- Do the parental sound-bites you run in your head lift you up or hold you down?
- Do you find yourself behaving in a counter-productive way and think 'That's just like my mother,' or 'That's just like my father'?

- How does viewing the world from the perspective of your parent state impact on attaining your goals?
- If the feelings, actions and thoughts of your parental state are not helping then what might you replace them with?
- What small changes would make a difference?

In the **Child** state we feel, act and think in similar ways to when we were children. There are two child aspects: the **adapted child** and **natural child**. The former shows a strong influence from its upbringing, and so relates to the parent state. The adapted child may be very obedient but manipulative, seeking to work around 'the rules', which gives rise to guilt. You may also see it as a positive thing to retain a childlike appreciation of the world as the natural child is the source of creation, recreation and spontaneity. The natural child may also be undisciplined and demanding. You will probably notice the similarity with the Id.

Consider how you feel, act and think based on your inner child's view of the world (or your perception of it). As always, write down your answers.

- How does your child state impact on your confidence?
- How does viewing the world from the perspective of your child state impact on attaining your goals?
- Do you find yourself behaving in a counter-productive way and think 'I know I'm being childish but . . .'? What might you do instead?
- If the feelings, actions and thoughts of your child state are not helping then what might you replace them with?
- What small changes would make a difference?

In the **Adult** state we tend towards a more objective view of reality. It's the voice of reason. It doesn't automatically react but it collects information, analyses it and works out options. It concentrates on considering all the facts and perspectives rather than pre-judging and jumping to conclusions. It deals more in the 'here and now', seeking solutions rather than dredging up past hurts and emotional baggage.

Using the 0–10 scale, rate the extent to which you behave in an adult state, where 0 equals 'not at all' and 10 equals 'all the time'. Use any point on the scale to reflect your opinion.

0	1	2	3	4	5	6	7	8	9	10

Not at all   Moderately   All the time

- How do you know you are at this point on the scale and not a point lower?
- What is it that has helped you to get from 0 to where you are now?
- What can you imagine doing if you move one point up the scale?
- What other adult-state attitudes would be beneficial for you to adopt?
- How would adopting these adult-state attitudes benefit you?
- What is one thing you could do over the next week that demonstrates adult-state attitudes?

Sometimes we find ourselves habitually doing things and don't necessarily know why, such as having a tantrum, 'throwing our toys out of the pram' and 'cutting our nose off to spite our face'. Sometimes it's a knee-jerk reaction in the heat of the moment. It's not necessary to undergo years of therapy to uncover the deep-seated motivations. Indeed, that may take a lifetime. A more productive response is first to find a way that interrupts the pattern. It may be as easy as 'counting to ten'. Then consider what would be a more productive response to a situation, one that fits in with your goals and values. A tantrum is a short-term, unproductive response to a situation. What would you do if you were considering the long game? What would be the most productive thing you could do that would still keep you on track for your future desired outcomes? Then just do these instead.

Three Selves

According to humanistic psychologist and therapist Carl Rogers, defence mechanisms prevent the self from growing and are the means by which we deny reality. He suggested we have three selves: the **real self**, the **imagined self** and the **ideal self**.

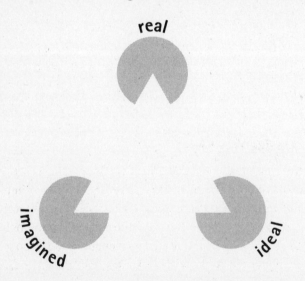

The Three Selves Triangle

The greater the gap between the imagined self and reality, the greater the likelihood of anxiety. Similarly, the greater the gap between the real self and the ideal self the more likely we are to experience anxiety. The same applies to the gap between the imagined self and the ideal self. This is not the basis on which to build confidence. Dealing with our defence mechanisms deals with the gap between imagined self and reality. Setting realistic and achievable goals that stretch us but do not overwhelm us is the way to bridge the gap between the real self and the ideal self.

Now consider what new information you can add to the background research for your one-minute promo?

One-Minute Promo

Additional thoughts, feelings and actions:

Review: Finding Your Keys

Review the *Confidence-Karma Chain* in Chapter 1 to see how the things we have considered in this chapter relate to other aspects of confidence building. It has focused on needs, perspectives and defence mechanisms, as well as the characteristics and behaviours for reaching one's full potential. The chapter has also explored the link in the chain to do with attitudes and values and personal identity (self-image). Take time to consider the review questions and write your answers in your journal.

- How do you rate your confidence at the conclusion of this chapter?
- What's better for you in terms of confidence?
- What have been the most effective aspects of this chapter in taking you forward?

- What knock-on effects do you imagine there will be when
  you put the information in this chapter into practice?

Karma Call

Consider how these new insights can help you to build confidence
in others. Write down three affirmative actions you will take to
continue the process. What will you pass on to other people in your
life? 'In order to see changes, what changes will you be?'

1.

2.

3.

In the next chapter, we explore the subject of building resilience
with practical exercises to tackle your inner critic.

Chapter 7

Being Hardy: Battling Demons and Building Resilience

Until one is committed, there is hesitancy, the chance to draw back, always ineffectiveness, concerning all acts of initiation and creation.

Johann Wolfgang von Goethe, 1749–1832, writer

Preview

In this chapter we consider resistance to change and tools for building resilience, explanatory styles for what happens in the world, and coping. It includes tools and techniques for editing and re-scripting unwanted thoughts and the negative ways in which we can talk to ourselves.

Psyching Yourself Up or Knocking Yourself Down?

There's an old saying, 'Sticks and stones will break my bones but names can never hurt me.' Anyone who has been on the receiving end of a verbal assault will know that this is not true. They may not break bones but words exert a powerful force on our health and well-being. Words and thoughts can inspire us, leave us feeling elated, or leave us defeated and deflated. They shape our view of the world and impact on how we feel about the world, how we view the world and what we do in the world. This chapter continues the theme of working on attitudes, considering coping styles and how we explain our successes and 'failures', and how we can change our words and thoughts to support better outcomes.

Coping with Change

When we are faced with change, our ability to cope depends on our psychological hardiness (similar to resilience). Rather than a personality characteristic it's more of a personality style or way of viewing the world. Whereas personality characteristics appear fixed, views can be changed. A core part of the life-coaching process is to consider alternative viewpoints and to offer opportunities to change attitudes.

The concept of psychological hardiness was proposed by social psychologists Suzanne Kobasa and Salvatore Maddi. It comprises three attitudes – the three Cs: **commitment**, **control**, and **challenge**. Individuals 'high in hardiness' are more likely to put stressful events into perspective and tend to perceive them as less of a threat and more of a challenge providing opportunities for personal development. As a consequence, stressful events are less likely to impact negatively on the health of a psychologically hardy person's health.

The buffering effect of psychological hardiness on health and well-being has been well researched and has been demonstrated in a wide variety of occupational groups, from business executives to students, including people working in highly stressful situations such as fire-fighters and people in the military. Let's consider the three Cs in turn:

- **Commitment** involves taking a genuine interest in other people and having a curiosity about the world and getting involved with people and activities. The opposite of commitment is **alienation**, which involves cutting yourself off and distancing yourself from other people.
- **Control** is the tendency to hold the attitude that control is something that comes from the inside and act as if you can influence the events taking place around you by your

own efforts. The opposite of control is **powerlessness** which includes the perception that your life is controlled by external forces (fate, government) and that you do not have the means or capabilities to achieve your goals. Our sense of control is often based on perception rather than objective facts.

- **Challenge** involves accepting that change is the norm, as opposed to stability, and that change offers opportunities for personal development rather than threats. The opposite of challenge is **security**, and the need for everything to stay familiar and predictable, allowing you to remain in your comfort zone

The Hardiness Triangle

Taken together, the three components of psychological hardiness provide the motivation and confidence to look to the future to find meaning in life, rather than seeking to repeat the past. Often in coaching we find that small changes can have a big impact. This is one of the basic tenets of the type of solution-focused coaching that I practise.

Building psychological hardiness need not be a mammoth task. It may involve simple ways in which we can reconnect with people or what some people call 'getting yourself out of the house'. A few minutes engaged in a chat at the bus stop is a whole lot better than hours at home spent going over our problems. A small change can cause a dramatic shift in perspective. Just by focusing on the small areas that we have control of and exercising that control may lead to fresh insights. Just choosing to break a routine and doing something slightly differently or in another order can cause a shift. We can build on the smallest of shifts in coaching. The same applies to challenges. We all crave predictability in life but at the same time we appreciate the difference a bit of novelty brings. Again, a small 'shake-up' may be all that it takes to open up a new perspective.

Adopting the three attitudes of hardiness (commitment, control, challenge) has been shown in research to enhance performance and health even in the face of stressful life changes. To choose the unfamiliar future over the familiar past also requires courage. So for confidence building, adopting these three attitudes creates a more future-oriented state of readiness.

Rating Hardiness Attitudes

Let's consider how you rate yourself for these three attitudes, using the 0–10 scale, where 0 equals 'lowest' and 10 equals 'highest'. Use any point on the scale that most accurately reflects your attitude. Review the three definitions above.

1. How would you rate yourself on commitment?

0	1	2	3	4	5	6	7	8	9	10

Low   Moderate   High

Now consider these questions:

- How have you got this far along the scale?
- What is it that has helped you to get from 0 to where you are now?
- If you are at 0, what would you imagine doing when the score is 1 or 2?
- What do you imagine doing if you move one point up the scale?
- What small, significant action will you commit to this week?
- What might you do right now?

2. How would you rate yourself on control?

0	1	2	3	4	5	6	7	8	9	10

Low   Moderate   High

Now consider these questions:

- How have you got this far along the scale?
- What is it that has helped you to get from 0 to where you are now?
- If you are at 0, what would you imagine doing when the score is 1 or 2?
- What do you imagine doing if you move one point up the scale?
- What small, significant action will you take control of this week to see how it moves your score on?

- What might you do right now?

3. How would you rate yourself on challenge?

0	1	2	3	4	5	6	7	8	9	10

Lower   Moderate   Higher

Now consider these questions:

- How have you got this far along the scale?
- What is it that has helped you to get from 0 to where you are now?
- If you are at 0, what would you imagine doing when the score is 1 or 2?
- What can you imagine doing if you move one point up the scale?
- What small, significant challenge will you take action on this week?
- What might you do right now?

Continue to look for opportunities to take small actions to demonstrate the attitudes of commitment, control and challenge in your life. Also consider what score would be 'good enough' for you to feel that the attitude changes are having a significant impact on your confidence building.

Coping Styles

From an early age we are taught how to replace negative emotions with positive ones. For children, gifts of sweets help 'heal' a disappointment or offer an 'antidote' to sadness, and sometimes even physical hurt. Fall off your bike and a chocolate bar will 'make it better'. Negative emotions can effectively put us on auto-pilot so that we act in quick, habitual ways to relieve the symptoms.

As adults we tend to use the same approach, for example with comfort eating: a slice of cheesecake is thought to cure all manner of emotional ills. This is known as **emotion-focused coping**. We focus on replacing the unpleasant emotions rather than getting to the root of the problem (**control-focused coping**). So, if we are sad or bored, we eat. When we gain weight and feel even more sad, we eat again to get rid of the unpleasant emotion, and on it goes. It's the same for people who go out and spend on their credit cards to get over their dismay at the size of their credit card bill!

This approach never gets to the root of the problem. Instead of dealing with the issues that cause the unpleasant emotions we blot those emotions out by drinking, eating cake, taking drugs or having sex. It's a short-term term fix rather than a long-term solution.

What we term **addictive personality** is more accurately a style of coping with negative emotions, using short-term fixes. It's learned behaviour not a deep-seated personality issue. For a longer-term fix, we need to address the underlying issues and take a control-focused or solution-focused approach. This is not to dismiss the emotional suffering. People may indeed need therapeutic help but it should be aimed at empowering them to learn new ways of coping rather than encumbering them with a label, which blocks the possibility for change.

Accepting (and embracing) the identity of 'addict' has an immediate knock-on effect on skills and strengths in the *Confidence-Karma Chain*. The same can be said for rejecting a 'victim' label and embracing that of 'survivor'. Stresses in the environment control our feelings, actions and thoughts. These become our attitudes, which frame our skills, and so on. If we want to address emotional issues, we work at influencing the environment in some way and also take control of our attitudes. Attitudes and values are things which are always within our control. So instead of resorting to emotion-focused coping as a long-term strategy, the first steps are to look for the opportunity rather than seeing problems as unbearable.

Consider what changes you can make, however small. Keep an eye on the long-term perspective, consider the broader context, develop realistic and achievable goals and take action on them. Much of *Confidence Karma* is about taking pre-emptive action, such as taking care of your general health and well-being, as well as looking outwards and giving something to others. What other things, however small, might you do to take back control of your confidence?

Dealing with Overwhelm

At times in our lives we can be faced with a heap of tasks that seems insurmountable. It's one big amorphous pile of potential misery with not enough hours in the day to tackle it. Invariably this seemingly unmanageable heap is usually made up of smaller heaps that are reasonably manageable but which we'd just prefer not to do. It's not that we're lazy, it's just that we're experiencing cognitive overload. There's just too much information to take in. We simply can't process the enormity of the task and so we don't bother. We just sit there and look at it. We protest that we don't have enough time to do everything and at the same time we don't do anything at all. Cognitive overload distorts our perception of time. We imagine it will take 'for ever'.

What we need is objective data to break the cycle. You can begin by breaking the amorphous heap into smaller pieces. It doesn't make the task any more appealing, just manageable. Pick one part of the task, set a timer and do it. Make a note of this timing to keep for future reference. Repeat the process with all the other subtasks. You now have objective data on how long the whole task and its component parts take instead of the very subjective 'for ever'. Undoubtedly you will discover that the smaller tasks are completed much quicker than you expect, as will be the huge tasks.

I use this approach when marking large numbers of student essays. A pile of 200 essays looks very daunting. So I split them into batches of five and put the big pile out of sight. They never take as long to mark as I first think they will. You can apply this approach to housework, gardening, office work, washing up the dinner things and even the ironing. It's exactly the same approach we should take for setting goals. Try this out and see how it works for you. What other examples can you think of in your life where this approach might work?

You Don't Have to Like the Choices, Just Pick One

Rarely in life are there situations with no choices whatsoever. However, sometimes we may feel caught between the proverbial rock and a hard place. There are choices, it's just that we don't like any of them. It feels like a lose–lose situation. So what are we to do?

- Begin by changing your attitude and acknowledge that although the choices are far from ideal, they are still choices.
- Enlist the help of a trusted friend and brainstorm all possible options, however ridiculous and fanciful. Don't censor, just come up with loads of ideas. Often we censor prematurely. This closes down options. It may be that the ridiculous idea contains something that sparkles, a faint glimmer that we can build on. Sometimes a silly idea will spark a train of thought that leads to something realistic and practical. If the exercise starts to become fun, this reduces tension and we think better when we are relaxed.
- Write down as many ideas as you can. Then read back the list and see if you can add a bit more detail. Other ideas

may occur to you while you are doing this, so write those down too.
- Once you have your list, go through each idea and ask 'How might this work?'
- Follow up with 'What aspect of this might work?'
- Then go through the list and discount any that definitely wouldn't work.
- Of those remaining, evaluate each one to see which might work best. It may still end up being 'the rock' or 'the hard place', but instead of reacting from pure emotion, you also have the perspective of logic.
- It will also get you into the habit of opening out and looking for possibility rather than immediately closing down.
- Consider other areas of your life to which you might apply this technique.

Next, I'd like us to consider one of the most common negative emotions we experience: boredom. A sure-fire antidote to boredom is to stop being boring. Yes, it's a little harsh but nothing blocks our goals more than choosing to do nothing else instead.

Dicing with Boredom

You're only bored because you aren't doing anything that you're really interested in at that moment! So rather than stick to familiar 'time-wasting' strategies (like TV channel surfing or moaning on social networking sites), here's a little technique that helps make up your mind to do something different. I've borrowed the idea from the book *The Dice Man* by Luke Rhinehart. It's the story of a therapist who decides to live his life according to the roll of dice, with alarming consequences. However, we are only going to subject our boredom to chance, not the whole of our lives.

Dice Technique

Make a list from 1 to 21 of the things you could be doing to relieve the boredom, that doesn't include food, drink or TV (or any other of your rituals). The reason it's 21 things is because that's the number of combinations on a pair of dice (1 & 1, 1 & 2, 1 & 3 . . . and so on up to 5 & 6 and 6 & 6). Include seven things you have been putting off, such as 'de-cluttering your wardrobe', and seven personal challenges that you never seem to make time for, such as 'learn a new language'. The remaining seven can be things you like doing to relax, such as 'go for a walk' or 'read a book', and so on.

The next time you feel bored and find your fingers zapping the remote control or opening and closing the fridge door, reach for a pair of dice and your list. Roll the dice and do whatever number is on your list. No excuses, no second roll. Just do it. Afterwards review your thoughts and feelings. Did it do the trick and relieve your boredom? If not, then roll again and try something else.

The dice technique is a fun way to break up boredom patterns and to get us to consider other options. However, it is no substitute for making informed choices and adopting a control-focused coping style, seeking to tackle the problem at its cause, not just mop up the symptoms. How else might you take control and deal with boredom?

Next we consider the lenses through which we view our lives.

Are Optimists Born or Made?

There is no such thing as a born pessimist or born optimist. Both are learned styles of explaining the world. So instead of saying 'I am a pessimist,' it's more accurate to say 'I adopt a pessimistic explanatory style.' We can unlearn that pessimistic style and re-learn an optimistic one. This is supported by decades of research by pioneering Positive Psychologist Martin Seligman. He has identified three key ingredients to the way we explain the world and our self-efficacy, that is how effective we see ourselves at being able to make changes in our lives. These are:

- **Making it personal** – it's all about me.
- **Making it permanent** – it'll never end.
- **Making it pervasive** – it affects everything.

The Explanatory Style Triangle

Let's see how the three ingredients of **personalization**, **permanence** and **pervasiveness** play out in their explanatory styles for positive and negative outcomes.

Personalization

When faced with a negative outcome, the pessimist takes it personally, whereas the optimist looks for context.

Negative Outcome

You've just competed for an employee of the month award and didn't get it (negative outcome). Let's compare two opposing responses:

- **Pessimistic explanation:** It was all my fault. I'm useless.
- **Optimistic alternative:** Other factors or people had an influence on this.

Think of a negative outcome in your life. Did you totally personalize it or did you consider the bigger picture? How might the optimistic explanation impact on confidence, self-esteem and self-efficacy, compared with the pessimistic style?

Positive Outcome

You've just been successful in a job interview and are offered the job. Consider which response would be closest to yours?

- **Pessimistic explanation:** It was fate. It was luck. The other candidates were really crap. They were desperate.
- **Optimistic alternative:** I'm good in interviews. It was down to my hard work. I did my homework. It was down to my personal qualities.

Think of a positive outcome in your life. Did you take any credit or dismiss your efforts outright?

Research has shown that there is a link between depression and explanatory style. People who dismiss positive outcomes as chance or luck and blame themselves for negative outcomes are more likely to experience depression. If you're explaining the world in a style that's related to depression, how will this impact on your self-confidence, esteem and efficacy? This is not to say that we should 'pass the buck'. Adopting an optimistic style means considering the outcome from more than just your own perspective. Unsupported self-blaming serves no function except to drag us down. It's not difficult to see how it fosters helplessness instead of hopefulness. So from now on monitor the degree to which you personalize your negative outcomes and depersonalize your successes. Consider other factors that contradict this view.

Permanence

Inevitably we all have 'good days' and 'bad days' but how we explain them counts towards our sense of hopefulness or helplessness. Do you put the day into perspective or view it as 'proof' of a permanent state of affairs?

Negative Outcome

Imagine you've had a bad day at work and uncharacteristically you've made some mistakes on an important job. Which response would be closest to yours?

- **Pessimistic explanation:** I'm finished. This is the beginning of the end.
- **Optimist alternative:** I was tired, I just had a bad day.

The pessimistic view makes it permanent whereas the optimistic view sees it as temporary and therefore can make it right. Again, consider how the pessimistic (helpless) view impacts on confidence, esteem and efficacy, compared with the optimistic (hopeful) view. What's your initial response when you have a bad day?

Positive Outcome

Imagine you successfully secure funding for a community project. Which response is closest to your likely, immediate response?

- **Pessimistic explanation:** I got lucky. They're giving money away to anyone these days.
- **Optimistic alternative:** I submitted a strong proposal, I get results.

If you think these responses seem unrealistic, I can tell you I hear similar things all the time in coaching. I've also heard the same things from students who've done well at exams ('the right questions came up' as opposed to 'I prepared for this exam really well'). The pessimistic view dismisses success as temporary and the optimistic view focuses on talents. Again, how might these two opposing explanatory styles impact on confidence building, esteem and efficacy?

Pervasiveness

This is all about distinguishing between specific situations and universal (general) rules. Again let's consider positive and negative outcomes and how pessimistic and optimistic explanations differ.

Negative Outcome
You fancy someone, ask them out for a coffee and they turn you down.

- **Pessimistic explanation:** They said no because I'm physically repulsive and have nothing to offer.
- **Optimist alternative:** I'm just not their type. I'm not attractive to that person.

The pessimistic (universal) explanation goes way beyond the evidence, whereas the optimistic (specific) explanation puts it into perspective. Again we see how the pessimistic explanation doesn't offer any hope that things will be different at another time, another place and with another person. The optimistic explanation does. Again, consider which one would be closer to your response. How might the two opposing explanations impact on confidence, esteem and efficacy?

Positive Outcome

You fancy someone and ask them out for a coffee and they accept.

- **Pessimistic explanation:** What's wrong with this person? This person must be a weirdo or desperate.
- **Optimist alternative:** I'm good company. I put people at ease. I have a lot to offer.

As usual, the pessimistic explanation is a no-win view and makes it all about specifics. The optimistic view generalizes, that is, 'I'm generally good company.' The optimistic view means a person is more likely to try again. The pessimistic explanation means a person is less likely to do so. Consider again which response is closer to one you might give? Consider the impact on confidence, esteem and efficacy.

Overall the implications of these three explanatory styles (attitudes) on confidence become clear. The pessimistic style demonstrates auto-prejudice in action and priming us for 'doing nothing', because 'there's no point in bothering'. The optimistic style is a far more powerful catalyst for action. Being optimistic is not about abdicating responsibility, it's about considering a broader range of options and giving ourselves credit where credit is due and also giving ourselves the benefit of the doubt.

Inner Critic Versus Inner Coach

Many of us are victimized by an emotional bully. Unfortunately it's one within ourselves: our own self-talk, the inner dialogue that offers a running commentary on our lives, and often doesn't offer a balanced view. Self-talk can be stock phrases and whole scripts that represent our inner attitudes. They impose limits on our actions and impact on our self-image, self-esteem and self-efficacy. More often, our self-talk is an inner critic. We internalize the negative feedback from significant people in our lives and habitually run and re-run these scripts. However, like any habit, it is possible to kick it and replace it with something more life-affirming. A few years ago, I realized that if anyone spoke to me like I spoke to myself, I would never speak to them again. If anyone on a social network sent me just one such message, they would be 'unfriended' in a heartbeat. So are you more in contact with your inner critic than your inner coach? Let's find out.

Monitoring Your Self-Talk

Any change should begin with an assessment of the data.

- Over the next week, keep a note of your self-talk. The aim is not to analyse it or try to change it. Just make a note of the words and the situation at the time. That's all.
- At the end of the week get two different coloured pens. With one circle all the positive key words, and with the other pen circle the negative key words.
- Are there more positive or more negative key words?
- Go back and rate the intensity of the positive words on a scale of 1–10, where 1 equals slight positive and 10 equals extremely positive.
- Do the same for the negative words, and rate them using the 1–10 scale, where 1 equals slightly negative and 10 equals extremely negative.
- Overall are you building yourself up or knocking yourself down?
- Now look for recurring patterns. Which words, phrases, statements are you using a lot?
- Write three statements that reflect the themes of your self-talk, using the words you routinely use. Think of these as your catchphrases (not only famous people have them).

Three most positive catchphrases:	Three most negative catchphrases:
1.	1.
2.	2.
3.	3.

The aim is to reduce the frequency of negative statements and their intensity. At the same time, increasing the frequency of positive statements and their intensity leads to self-talk that is more uplifting. Let's begin with the positive statements.

Enhancing Positive Self-Talk

Under what conditions do you say positive things to yourself? What are the circumstances? How might you maximize the chances of saying these things more often? Where would you be, what would you do? Who would be there with you? It may be useful to review Chapter 2 and your skills and strengths, and the situations when you reported increased confidence ratings.

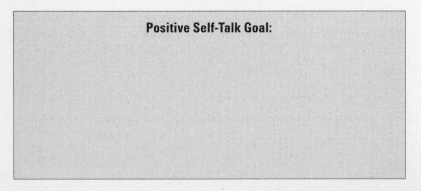

Positive Self-Talk Goal:

- Repeat this for all of your positive statements.
- Maybe you have a positive statement that you would like to say to yourself. What would this be, and under what conditions would it be most likely to happen? Make this another positive self-talk goal. Repeat for as many positive statements as you wish.
- Now take actions on these before moving on to look at negative self-talk, as these actions can act as an emotional buffer. This will also put you in a more positive frame of mind to deal with the negative stuff.

Rewriting Negative Scripts

Our inner critic is like our alarm system. It aims to protect us from harm and may contain words and phrases from our upbringing such as 'Don't run before you can walk.' We might think of our inner critic as a well-meaning but pessimistic, tactless, curmudgeonly elderly relative. Whenever we step outside our comfort zone, our inner critic blurts out 'stock phrases' designed to stop us in our tracks. It also has the tendency to be blunt and to berate us after the event, so that we won't repeat the mistake, and keeps reminding us of our shortcomings as well.

The words we use to describe, praise or scold ourselves form part of our self-fulfilling prophecies. We begin to look for supporting evidence no matter how faulty the original assumption. The next step is to take action to neutralize, re-educate and re-script that inner voice and change the dialogue from inner critic to inner coach.

- Consider the most negative things that you say to yourself from the data collection exercise. If a stranger spoke to you like that or someone posted this as a comment on a social networking site, what would you do? Would you want to be friends with that person any more?

- Choose your three most negative statements and be your own editor. How might you rephrase them?
- Think of a person who has or who had a very positive influence in your life. How would they be likely to re-phrase the statement? Remember, they are trying to be kind and spare your feelings.
- Is your statement a gross exaggeration? What would be something more realistic?

Negative statements	Re-scripted statements
1.	1.
2.	2.
3.	3.

- Over the next week when you catch yourself, using the negative statement, say 'That's harsh. I'll rephrase that,' and say the alternative re-scripted statement.
- Replace the malevolent with the benevolent.
- At the end of the week's trial, what's the verdict?

The language we use indicates our level of self-esteem and maintains it at that level. So if you have to berate yourself, turn it into feedback with the aim of moving yourself forward, and do so with politeness and civility.

Exercise

What changes to your negative self-talk would have the most impact on your confidence? What tells you that you are able to implement these changes? What else could you do to quieten your inner critic and amplify your inner coach?

Editing for Optimism – Ditch the Judgements

Putting ourselves down usually includes judgements fuelled by anger. We are angry that something didn't turn out, we blame ourselves and we tend to generalize and exaggerate. So we'll use phrases like 'totally useless', 'absolute rubbish' and 'crap'. The minute you've blurted out something negative, take a deep breath and rephrase. Aim for something objective and neutral. Instead of saying 'I'm such a dirty, lazy slob,' consider 'I'm not very good at keeping things tidy,' and then 'Keeping things tidy is not one of my strongest skills.' 'Dirty, lazy slob' operates at the level of identity, so in the *Confidence-Karma Chain* it influences skills and strengths. Dirty, lazy slobs are unlikely to develop those skills and so the possibility of change is blocked. So why bother? In Chapter 2 we considered the idea that we can't be brilliant at everything, so it might be time to hire a cleaner or swap skills with someone. Alternatively you can decide what is 'good enough' for you. You may not want to be the best 'tidier-upper' in the history of the world ever. A satisfactory, workable level of skill may be all you need. It's also important to look out for words you use that impose limits, such as 'I'll never get the hang of this.' It could be that things are taking longer than expected, but that doesn't necessarily mean 'never'. So say 'It's taking me longer than I expected to get the hang of this.' Again this provides the possibility for improvement. This leads to the second point.

Stop Exaggerating

Do you habitually exaggerate negative states? Are you likely to claim devastation rather than frustration when something goes wrong? Do you claim to be 'absolutely gutted' when you're just disappointed? When you're thirsty are you 'dying for a drink'? I've heard someone who missed their mid-morning snack and claim to be 'literally dying of hunger' at lunch time, even though they'd eaten breakfast. Psychological research demonstrates that changes to the wording of our questions and statements can yield different results and actually cause us to add extra non-factual details to match the question or statement. If the question uses emotive words, the responses tend to be more 'over the top'. So consider some of your habitual hyperbole, that is your tendency to overstate the case for dramatic effect, then bring it back to reality.

Exercise

For the next seven days, make an effort to be more accurate about your emotional states, feelings and achievements. If in doubt inflate the positives by 10% and discount the negatives by 10%. Invite a friend to try this out too and, at the end of the week, compare notes. Consider how your choice of language affects your mood, confidence and esteem.

Up Until Now

Every time you find yourself making absolute, permanent statements, closing off any possibility of change, add the words 'up until now' at the end of the sentence, then put the sentence into the past tense. So, for example, 'I'm rubbish at keeping things tidy' becomes 'I *have been* rubbish at keeping things tidy . . . *up until now.*' Better still 'I haven't been good at keeping things tidy, up until now.' This in turn becomes 'Keeping things tidy is not one of my strongest skills up until now.' Again, it opens up the possibility of change.

Part of Me

To change your perspective on strong emotions you can create a subtle shift by replacing the 'I am' with 'part of me is'. For example, replace 'I am angry,' with 'Part of me is angry,' and 'I am depressed,' with 'Part of me is depressed.' This makes the emotion sound less 'all-consuming'. It sounds less like your identity and more like a temporary state as it injects perspective and reason into the emotional response. It's a way of still owning an emotion but not letting it be all-encompassing and overwhelming. Can you ask questions of the parts of you that are not gripped by the emotion? Try it yourself and see how the two statements feel.

Exercise

Consider some of your negative self-talk that closes down options for you. Using the techniques above, rewrite the self-talk. What options do you have to set goals to take you forward? Write down as many options for goals as you can.

All of these techniques transform your inner criticism into constructive feedback. They also re-open the idea that things might change. On this basis, we have an opportunity to set goals (*see Chapter 9*). In the next chapter we consider how to create more affirmative self-talk; meanwhile next we consider negative thoughts and how to get the better of them.

Automatic Negative Thoughts

Sometimes negative thoughts appear to 'pop into our heads' often unwanted and uninvited. Therapist Aaron Beck refers to these as **automatic negative thoughts** (ANTs). Thoughts of unworthiness, helplessness or failure are all common examples. The tendency to rehearse these thoughts over and over again is known as rumination. It's the psychological equivalent of the bovine digestion process, 'chewing the cud'. Cows keep bringing their food back up and having another go at chewing it, over and over again. ANTs and the process of rumination have the effect of lowering confidence, esteem and efficacy. If we allow the cycle to continue, our pattern-seeking brain seeks out more evidence to support the thoughts. To break this vicious cycle we need to challenge those automatic negative thoughts as they occur.

Firstly we need a signal to interrupt the process. One method used in **Cognitive–Behavioural Therapy** (CBT) is to put an elastic band around the wrist. When a negative thought (or negative self-talk) occurs, snap the elastic band against the wrist to create a mildly painful shock. In one counselling course I attended, we were all encouraged to shout out 'Foul!' (as in sport, not the poultry) whenever anyone said something to 'put themselves down'. We were then invited to rephrase it. Find a cue or method that works for you.

ANTs (and self-talk) tend to twist the facts, ignore the facts and go beyond the evidence. ANTs often do not hold up to scrutiny.

Cognitive Distortions and Logical Errors

Beck identifies a number of 'logical errors' or 'cognitive distortions' that unfavourably distort our perceptions of ourselves:

- **All-or-nothing, black-and-white thinking** – seeing situations in either/or terms with no middle ground. We discussed this in Chapter 2 when considering confidence highs and lows.
- **Catastrophizing** – a combination of exaggeration and pessimistic permanence. Making relatively minor things into 'the end of the world'.

- **Mind-reading** – when, despite a total lack of evidence, maybe just a hunch, you assume that you know what's going on in someone's head. Lots of everyday misunderstandings occur in this way. You may infer that someone doesn't like you or has a negative opinion of you.
- **Labelling** – when you confuse behaviour with the person. So instead of saying 'My performance wasn't very good on this occasion,' you say 'I'm no good.' It's similar to the personalization we considered in the pessimistic explanatory style.
- **Jumping to conclusions** – when you have a little bit of information and you infer far more from it than the evidence suggests, so that one late phone call means 'We're breaking up.'
- **Emotional reasoning** – where you confuse your feelings with the facts.

You'll have noticed the cross-over between these distortions and the communication tips in Chapter 4. Challenging negative thoughts with logical questioning exposes the distortions, which are often based on an incomplete picture, a flawed interpretation or a combination of the two.

Logical Disputing

Firstly, it is important to make a distinction between responsibility and blame. Knowing that your actions (or inaction) led to particular consequences is feedback. Responsibility is about taking ownership, whereas blame serves no useful function whatsoever. Secondly, it's good to get into the habit of considering mitigating circumstances and alternative causes. It helps make sure you are not taking responsibility for things over which you have no control. So pick a persistent automatic negative thought, such as 'I'm useless,' 'I'm just a screw-up,' 'I'm a lousy friend,' and so on.

Use the following questions to test the validity of the statement and expose the black-and-white thinking:

- What's the evidence for this negative thought?
- What evidence do you have to contradict this thought?
- What are the exceptions?
- What are the mitigating circumstances?
- How do things look from another perspective, such as that of an impartial observer?
- What evidence would a third person offer, to the contrary?
- What exceptions would this impartial observer see?

The aim of these questions is to get a more accurate, flexible, evidence-based evaluation of events. Logical disputing is useful to help find alternative explanations of outcomes. This also opens up more choices and thus creates a sense of hope.

Another Thought on Black-and-White Thinking

People who see things in terms of black and white tend to have a high personal need for structure in their lives. They tend to be intolerant of ambiguity and uncertainty. We are all drawn to quick and easy explanations, which sometimes leads to errors as we have discovered. Our pre-programmed tendency to seek simplicity encourages quick solutions, but often at the expense of accuracy. The central theme running through this chapter is the need for high quality data – black-and-white thinking will never deliver this.

As part of my work I consult on research projects and also teach research methods. When collecting data, we need to consider what form the measurement will take and how much detail it will include. This may range from simple categorization, to rank ordering, to taking an accurate measurement. The decision we make about the richness of the data measurement at the start will have profound effects when we come to analyse the results.

At the lowest level are basic categories. So for example in a race, the two basic categories are win or lose. We often apply these simple categories in life such as short/tall, fat/thin, clever/ stupid, confident/unconfident, and so on. The problem with these simple, general categories is that they provide very little detail. For instance, in a race, we have no idea who came in second or third. We just have one winner and a load of losers. So, if we take the level measurement up a notch, we put everyone in rank order (1st, 2nd, 3rd, and so on). This gives us more information and we can still work out the winners and losers. However, we have no idea how much faster one person was compared to others. So, if we take timings, we can work out the ranks and then the winners and losers. Richer information can be reduced to lower levels but not the other way round. The exercises in this chapter (and throughout the book) have all focused on getting better information. The fact is that we do actually possess the rich data, it's just that we choose not to use it. The aim for these exercises is to get you into the habit of basing your decisions on better information and so broadening your options. One other thing occurs to me. Taking the black-and-white view, we can label someone a 'loser' in a race even when they have surpassed their personal best. Black and white doesn't tell us that either.

From Esteem to Acceptance

In Chapter 1 we considered Windy Dryden's assertion that self-acceptance is preferable to self-esteem, comparing it to Carl Rogers's unconditional positive regard. So what if you considered that you're doing the best you can in life, given the circumstances and resources at your disposal? How would that help shift the nagging self-doubts? How would that alter your perceptions? Words come easy to our inner critic and positive inner attitudes sometimes take a bit of coaxing to bring out our inner coach, but it's well worth the effort. Positive inner attitudes in the form of affirmative self-talk can give us that all-important buoyancy resilience in life rather than having negative self-talk wear us down and drag us under. Inner attitudes like hardiness and optimism shape the outer aspects of our lives.

Something Else for the One-Minute Promo

Thoughts, feelings, attitudes and values:

Review: Finding Your Keys

Review the *Confidence-Karma Chain* in Chapter 1 to see how the things we have considered in this chapter relate to other aspects of confidence building. This chapter has focused on the values and attitudes, and thoughts and feelings links in the chain.

- How do you rate your confidence at the conclusion of this chapter?
- What's better for you in terms of confidence?
- What have been the most effective aspects of this chapter in taking you forward?
- What knock-on effects do you imagine there will be when you put the information in this chapter into practice?

Karma Call

How do these new insights help you to build confidence in others? Write down three affirmative actions you will take to continue the process. What will you pass on to other people in your life? In order to see changes, what changes will you be?

1.

2.

3.

In the next chapter, we explore the strategic use of the imagination. This includes creating more life-affirming self-talk and using visualization techniques to support your goals.

Chapter 8

Raising Aspirations, Part 1: Possibility Programming

We lift ourselves by our thought, we climb upon our vision of ourselves.

Orison Swett Marden, 1850–1924, writer

Preview

In this chapter we consider a series of tools and techniques to begin the process of raising aspirations and paving the way for your goal-setting. We explore how to use the power of the imagination strategically to support personal development, including confidence building. The chapter also offers the means to create affirmative statements to counter negative inner dialogue.

Words and Pictures

A fundamental aspect of being human is our creativity. This capacity can be self-defeating or life-affirming. Every act of creation begins with a thought and this chapter offers the keys to tune our thoughts in support of positive life changes. It builds on the relaxation and mindfulness exercises in Chapter 3 and prepares the way for your goal setting in the next chapter, in which you 'climb on your vision of yourself'. Seizing control of the words and pictures that you use to describe your life and your future is a key step in creating lasting positive change.

Self-Affirming Self-Talk

One way to neutralize negative self-talk is to write your own positive self-talk in the form of affirmations. These are carefully worded positive statements that you deliberately repeat to yourself. You can use one of these like a mantra so you can incorporate it in your meditation practice. The one-word mantra 'calmer' is the simplest affirmation. Mantras provide alternatives to self-talk and help to support goals, including confidence building.

How to Write Affirmations

The aim of affirmations is to support attitude change. To achieve this, they need to be persuasive and believable, so just ignore advice that tells you to repeat unrealistic statements. For confidence building, you wouldn't start with 'I am the most confident person in the universe and I can achieve anything I set my mind to.' The simple rebuttal to this is 'Where's the evidence?' So let's consider ways to make your affirmations persuasive but still grounded on planet Earth. Perhaps the most famous affirmation was coined by French pharmacist Émile Coué: 'Every day in every way I'm getting better and better.' It has some merits but is rather vague. What does 'every way' mean? Also in what ways is he getting better? Better from an illness, better at shoplifting, better at self-delusion or better from efforts at personal development? Here are some simple rules to follow for creating really effective affirmations.

- **Affirmations should be positively stated.** They are called affirmations because they are affirmative statements. That's where the Coué affirmation got it right, even if it is vague. Affirmations should not include 'not'. If it's phrased in the negative, we first process the positive and then negate. It works on the same principle as 'Don't think about pink elephants.' By the time you've worked out what not to think, you've already thought it. So instead of saying 'I am not eating junk food from now on,' say 'Every day the percentage of healthy foods I eat increases.'

- **Affirmations should be believable.** This makes them less likely to be objectively refuted by your inner critic. Remember that some of your affirmations may contradict your negative self-talk. So if the affirmation is too far removed from the put-down it will be rejected. A more subtle approach is to state the affirmation in terms of continual improvement so it contains the sense that change has already begun. It's not so glamorous but 'My confidence is improving,' or 'Day by day I am becoming more confident,' are harder to reject than 'I am the living embodiment of confidence.' However, as there's nothing to say how this is happening, this leads us to the all-important action. The Coué affirmation isn't believable; 'every way' is too easy to challenge.
- **Affirmations should be action-oriented.** Link your affirmations to goals so that they don't just seem wishful thinking. Consider 'Every day with each goal-directed action my confidence is improving.' It's more difficult to dispute this. The Coué affirmation includes no sense of how the change is achieved.
- **Affirmations should be short and simple.** This way it takes less time to process them. Simple statements are less ambiguous and so less open to dispute by your inner critic. Long sentences with multiple clauses take longer to process and may contain conflicting elements. It might be possible to agree with some parts of the affirmation but not others. If it's contradictory, it will be rejected outright. Brief affirmations are more likely to be internalized. The Coué affirmation ticks this box.

- **Affirmations should be specific.** Make the affirmation particular to one thing rather than a vague, all-encompassing one. The Coué affirmation is too vague. It's more effective if you can link a specific change to a goal and an action. Rather than 'every way', it is better to write several specific, behaviour-based affirmations.
- **Affirmations should be personal.** The easiest way to do this is to link them to your goals. I find it helpful to write two versions. One statement is in the first person 'I am' and the other uses my name, followed by a statement in the second person. For instance, 'Day by day I am increasing the percentage of healthy foods in my diet,' followed by 'Day by day, Gary, you are increasing the percentage of healthy foods in your diet.' You may have noticed that 'healthy' is a very vague word. What could I use instead?

How to Use Your Affirmations

It helps to use affirmations in a variety of ways, just as we have looked at building confidence from different angles by addressing attitudes in different ways. So you could use them as part of your meditation practice, you could create notes to yourself and place them in strategic places, put them on screen savers, repeat them to yourself whilst on the treadmill in the gym or whilst out on a walk. Another method is to write them out ten times and say them out loud, three times a day. Later in the chapter we explore visualization techniques so consider combining affirmations with these.

Your Self-Talk as Raw Material

To counter our inner critic we need to re-script these stock phrases. So, rather than repeat a stream of unhelpful negative statements, we can replace them with our own affirmative, uplifting ones to bring out our inner coach.

Use the editing techniques from the previous chapter to challenge your self-talk, and use the guidelines above to create an affirmation. The aim is to create an antidote to the self-talk. Once you have converted the negative self-talk into more constructive feedback, it may suggest a goal as a means to address or neutralize the self-talk. So set the goal, write an affirmation to support it and take action on it.

Negative Self-Talk Phrase (Put-Down)	The Opposite/Antidote
1.	1.
2.	2.
3.	3.

A particular favourite amongst students is 'I'm sorry I'm being a bit thick; could you explain that again.' As the teacher I respond 'No you're not thick. We all learn differently and I haven't explained it in a way for you to grasp it yet. So try this.' The question gives me the opportunity to explain the concept in another way. This will most likely benefit other students and I learn something new too. Let's work with the 'I'm thick' example. We could re-script this as 'I have the sense and the courage to ask questions when I don't understand something.'

Real Life and Imagination

Imagination has something in common with confidence. We all have a capacity for it. It's not a gift bestowed on the chosen few either. Just like every other aspect of being human, imagination is not an all-or-nothing thing. Imagination is simply our ability to form words and pictures in our minds. Without it we would not be able to learn. It's just that the imagination of highly creative people seems to overshadow everyday imagination.

It requires imagination to connect the arrangement of the abstract markings on this page to meaningful concepts. We usually learn the alphabet by linking each letter with a picture. When we first learn to read the books contain a lot of pictures; as we progress, we begin to form our own mental pictures from the words. When we read we may even imagine what some of the characters are thinking or what their motivations may be. You may watch a film adaptation of a novel and be disappointed that the actor is wrong for the character or thrilled that he is just like you imagined he would look. If your mouth has ever watered when watching a cookery programme or just reading a recipe, if you've ever exaggerated or worried, or ever been scared of the dark, you have enough imagination for the exercises that follow.

Our brains (or bodies) do not easily distinguish between reality and fantasy. That is why we can be moved to tears, scared or sexually aroused simply by reading words on the printed page. We conjure up the mental images and our brain responds as if they were real experiences. The tools and techniques in this chapter help you to exploit this 'loophole' by setting an agenda for your imagination by strategically creating mental images. So what kind of things can you do with your imagination using the skills you already possess?

Creative Visualization

Creative visualization is the most frequently used term for the strategic use of the imagination. Visualization is the act of forming mental images, and changing them in some way is the creative bit. For instance, picture a dog. That's visualization. Now if you change the colour or turn it into a cartoon dog, that's creative visualization. It's not that different to what we do when we worry. The term has been criticized because it seems to have an emphasis on visual images. However, you can do the same with a sound, a feeling, a smell, a taste or an emotion. We all have a preference for different senses. So, with the following exercises, if your visual image isn't compelling, then just enhance it with any of the other senses. You may have also encountered the terms manifesting, or cosmic ordering or the law of attraction. All of these are basically visualization techniques but often without an imperative for action. The main difference is that we are using the techniques to support our actions and our goals. Some techniques are offered as a substitute for doing things in the real world. With confidence building, there is no substitute for doing.

Mental Rehearsal

Mental rehearsal has an emphasis on processes and skills. It is based on the old adage that says 'Practice makes perfect.' It involves creating mental motion pictures of you in particular situations actually doing something. As our brains find it difficult to distinguish between reality and imagination, skills practised mentally have similar beneficial effects to practice in the real world. It may sound fantastic but the most accomplished higher-level athletes use mental rehearsal to stay at the top of their game. For instance, a study has shown that basketball players who practised 'shooting hoops' in their imagination demonstrated almost as much improvement in accuracy as those who did so in real life. Similar findings have been found for other sports such as golf and football, and even with body-building. Artists, pilots, astronauts and surgeons routinely use mental rehearsal to support real-life practice to prepare themselves for challenges. The techniques are also used in psychological coaching and therapy, as well as to help with things such as exams and driving tests. Practising the skills in your imagination is like having your own personal driving simulator.

From a psychological perspective, the use of visualization techniques follows from the idea that 'We are defined by what we focus on.' Actively and strategically we retune our perception to positive outcomes, using pictures, sounds and other sensations. This prepares the way and gets us fit and ready for action.

Positive Worrying and the Placebo Effect

Many people are unaware that they use visualization techniques routinely, every time they worry. Whenever we do so, we imaginatively create and rehearse the worst. We replay images of past events ('if only'), re-living then over and over. We can even worry about things that have not yet happened, create images of future events ('what if') and play them over and over in our heads. This means we are well-practised visualizers. So, since we all know how to worry, it makes sense to transform this existing 'skill' into a strength. If we change the direction and tune into positive outcomes, our goals, then 'what if' and 'if only' become questions of possibility. From this perspective, visualization is just **positive worrying**. Studies have confirmed a beneficial effect of visualization and relaxation techniques when used in conjunction with traditional Western medicine. One theory is that they help to trigger the natural placebo response. (A placebo is a sugar pill used as part of the controlled clinical trials for new medicines. Despite the placebo containing no active medicinal ingredients a significant number of patients receiving sugar pills show an improvement in their medical conditions. People believe they are taking medicine which they expect to have a beneficial effect, and it does.) We still don't fully understand the placebo effect but it indicates strongly that the mind (imagination) can be used to impressive effect.

A key ingredient to maximize the efficacy of your visualization is how you approach it, that is, your attitude. You need to invest in the visualization with a positive mental attitude. Boost the effects by 'suspending your disbelief' and really 'acting into it'. So rather than saying to yourself 'Let's see *if* it works,' you need to say 'Let's see *how well* it works.' Not forgetting, of course, to play with visualization techniques and have fun with them. We are more creative when we relax.

Confidence Power Shower

This energizing visualization doesn't require any additional time investment. It's done in the shower. As you stand under the water, imagine a beautiful empowering, refreshing, energizing, invigorating light streaming from the shower-head (as well as the water). The light may be white, pink, golden or pale blue; you choose. Imagine this light-charged energy washing away the tiredness and charging you up for the day. The light activates your skills and strengths and inspires you to take action. Use whatever positive thought you wish. Do this every day for two weeks, or more if you wish. Assess the effects on you. You may also wish to repeat the process before going to bed. At this time you can switch the emphasis to creating a calming, cleansing (wash away the cares of the day) effect.

Use this experience as a basis for re-creating the whole experience in your imagination, whenever you choose. It just takes a few minutes to find a quiet place, close your eyes, do the breathing exercises and imagine the water washing away the negativity and the light sparking your confidence resources. Exaggerate, act into it and have fun with it. As with all of the personal experiments I suggest, the aim is simply to try things out to see how they work. Then reflect and adjust your approach until you have something that works well for you.

Here's another very simple technique that can be used through-out the day, or just before going to sleep.

Blue-White Light Visualization

- Get comfortable, close your eyes and count down from 10 to 1 on each abdominal breath.
- Now take another 10 abdominal breaths and on the inhalation imagine that you are breathing in a beautiful blue-white healing light.
- Imagine that the whole of your body lights up.
- Exhale all of your fears, worries and concerns. Let the light carry them away.
- On each breath let the light glow brighter and begin to extend outside your body until you are enveloped in an egg of blue-white light.
- Slowly let the light fade, knowing it will return any time you desire it.
- With your eyes still closed, try to smile inside without letting it show on your face.
- Count yourself back up from 1 to 10.

The next exercise also works well as a meditation and involves taking a familiar experience and exaggerating it for an improved relaxation effect.

Creating a Sanctuary

If you've ever listened to commercial relaxation and guided medi-tation CDs you'll know that the ideal scenes of tranquillity all seem to be beaches, meadows or forests. The music is often all gongs, flutes and wind chimes. Many people can relate to them as they appeal to popular experiences. However, none of it is much use if any of the components are your idea of a nightmare. The process is more effective when you are able to create your own relaxing scenes. It can be a real place, with a few personal adjustments, a number of experiences combined, or something totally from your imagination. Borrow from other places, mixing and matching to create something brand new. Again, play around with what works for you. It doesn't have to be perfect first time. I've used this exercise in courses and there's always one person who complains about an aspect of their sanctuary, such as they don't like the curtains. I just have to remind them 'It's your sanctuary and you are the designer. You are creating the curtains. If you don't like them, change them!'

Preparation

For this experiment consider the most relaxing environment you have ever experienced (or can imagine).

Technique

- Relax with some long, slow, deep breaths.
- Begin to picture your ideal place of relaxation.
- Focus on the sights, sounds, smells and textures.
- Think about your emotions at the time. How were you feeling?
- Imagine those sensations occurring in your body now.
- Keep adding detail to make the experience more vivid, more compelling, creating a place that you can retreat to and totally relax in. Focus on the key ingredients that have a relaxing effect and exaggerate them.
- Really act into the experience.
- Keep adding details until you feel as if you're there.
- Enjoy the experience.

Whatever the content of your ideal place the aim is to create a special sanctuary as vividly as possible. What better way is there to get to sleep at night than by going to your place of sanctuary? Try this every night for two weeks and note the effects it has on your day-to-day living, including your sleep.

Your Confidence Laboratory

Once you've spent time enjoying your place of sanctuary, in your imagination you can create a doorway, tunnel, portal or passageway that leads to your confidence laboratory. This is a place that you may use for finding solutions, either by yourself or with any advisors or experts you meet there. It can be anything you chose from a clinical-looking laboratory, to an old library, to a cave. It can be something space-age, something that feels magical or even just a dining room or the kitchen. The confidence laboratory is based on the idea that context is very important for learning. You are creating a context in which you feel empowered and in which things can happen.

- Relax with some long, slow, deep breaths.
- Begin by creating a room in your imagination. Just form the basic structure.
- Now begin adding detail. You are the interior designer so decorate it as you wish.
- Add soft furnishings, wallpaper, light boxes, favourite pictures and so on.
- Add any equipment you want, such as a computer, filing cabinets, a desk, sofas, or a big kitchen table. The choice is yours.
- Add anything that creates a confidence-building place. Maybe add gadgets, gym equipment, a music system, television displays and so on.
- Add a solution-finding generator, such as a cubicle you can sit in to use when you want to consider all options.
- Spend time adding the detail. The key thing is to create a sense of the kind of place where solutions will emerge. Once, you have created it you simply need to recall it next time. Of course, you can update it whenever you feel it is necessary.

> When you are happy with the details of the room focus on
> your dilemma and decision.

Focus on creating big, bright, fun images and add sounds and sensations too. You may find sounds create a more vivid experience of how everything feels. Work with whatever sense makes it more real to you. The more effort you put into creating a picture, the more impact it has and the more memorable it becomes. Just have fun with it and enjoy the practice. Do it to amuse yourself on a long train journey (but not behind the wheel of the car). You can go to your laboratory to run the following visualization exercises. You might even devise your own. So you begin by getting into a relaxed state, then going to your sanctuary and then to your lab. It all helps to intensify the visualization experiences.

Now that you have had an imagination work-out, let's consider how we can apply creative visualization techniques to the pursuit of your goals, that is to imagine your preferred personal positive outcomes.

Future Desired Confidence Outcomes

Part of the worrying process, when thinking about challenges, is agonizing over every little thing that can go wrong. It's our brain's overzealous way of preparing us for every eventuality. Unfortunately, it sometimes includes things that are highly improbable and sometimes impossible. Here's a technique for helping to create a compelling vision of your confidence-building actions. Instead of imagining everything that could possibly go wrong, just focus on the moment immediately after the end result. First, decide on a small, significant action that would move the confidence-building process along. Use the ideas you created in your definition of confidence in Chapter 1, My example would be of giving a presentation at work.

- Close your eyes and take some long, slow, deep breaths to get you into a relaxed state.
- In your imagination picture the scene immediately after you have taken your confidence action. Smile.
- Get a sense of how you are feeling. Really enjoy that feeling and act into the feeling, making it more real. You are really there in that moment.
- If other people are around you, have them smile and congratulate you too. Hear them say 'Well done.' Maybe you even get a round of applause.
- Let the sense of achievement build.
- Spend a few moments really enjoying the feeling.
- When you are ready, open your eyes, take some more slow deep breaths and go out and do it for real.

The idea behind this exercise is to create the sense in the mind of already having achieved the challenge. This is a particularly useful technique for dealing with nerves when speaking in public. You can adapt it for almost anything, such as a first date, although having lots of people around you smiling and saying 'Well done,' or shouting 'Bravo!' (with a standing ovation) is perhaps a step too far. Use whatever works for you.

As we have already discussed, imagination can be strategically employed to develop and enhance skills.

Mental Rehearsal Techniques

Mental rehearsal makes the same connections in the brain as if you were doing something for real. Try the technique with a routine task that you already do well, in this case making a cup of tea:

Basic Technique
- Take long, slow deep breaths to induce your relaxation response.

- Mentally experience yourself performing the task perfectly.
- Add details from all of your senses to create a vivid and compelling experience. Create a sense that you are actually there.
- Add context and detail. Add sounds and smells.
- It may also help to act out any gestures.
- Repeat the process with some different scenarios, such as doing your filing or a pile of ironing.

This simple technique allows you to gain the basic skills of mental rehearsal. As before, use your sense preference to make the 'experience' more vivid and compelling. When you are comfortable with the technique, move up to the next level and use it for a skill you want to improve, from playing a musical instrument to a sporting activity, learning to drive or mastering a tricky dance move.

Confidence Role Model Remote Viewing

For the purposes of this exercise, think of a new skill that you would like to improve, such as your tennis swing, yoga ability, driving skills or presentation skills. Now, think of a role model who excels at your chosen skill, and whom you have been able to observe in action. You may wish to break the task into component steps and practise each step in turn, before putting the steps together.

So here's the process:

- Breathe and relax.
- Mentally observe your role model performing the task, perfectly.
- Once you are satisfied with the experience you have created, have your role model step into your body and continue to let them guide your actions.

- Again, add details from all of your senses to create a vivid and compelling experience of performing the activity.
- Add the emotions you feel as you perform the task perfectly.
- Keep practising, over and over, in your imagination. Make it as real as the real thing.

When you are happy with this stage, it's time to go it alone, with your role model coaching from the sidelines.

Go it Alone

- Breathe and relax.
- This time you are performing the task perfectly, all on your own.
- You move your body just as your role model does.
- Experience your role model coaching you, supportively, from the sidelines.
- Again, add details from all of your senses to create a vivid and compelling experience.
- Add the emotions you feel as you perform the task perfectly.

Perform your chosen task whenever you get a spare minute, by adding the mental rehearsal to your relaxation practice.

Perfect Conversation

If you need to have a 'difficult conversation' with someone you can mentally rehearse a positive outcome to prepare the way.

- Take long, slow, deep breaths to induce your relaxation response.
- Create the scene in your imagination and see, feel and hear the conversation going well.

- The details of the conversation are not as important as the sense that you are having a calm conversation, listening to each other and appreciating each other's point of view.
- Jump to the end of the conversation and imagine you are parting and both saying 'I'm really glad we had this conversation.'

Of course, some conversations are more difficult than others, but if we start with a positive experience that it has already gone well, you begin in a more positive and relaxed state of mind.

Customize and Visualize

All of the techniques from this chapter and Chapter 3 can be performed in a few minutes, but if you have more time and wish to enhance the effects you can mix and match techniques to create a custom-made experience. Here are some suggestions.

Preparation

Consider a situation in which you feel you need more confidence.

- Go to your place of sanctuary and add the calmer confidence mantra.
- Go to your confidence lab and use any of your confidence-boosting equipment.
- Take a moment to experience the effects.
- Now visualize your future desired outcome, the moment after you've taken action, experiencing the positive responses and feelings.

When we encounter a problem we often seek the opinion of a trusted friend or even go to seek the advice of an expert. However, wouldn't it be great if you could enlist the help of any expert from the past, present or future?

Your Confidence Crew

Having a team of helpers that you can access in your imagination is about shifting perspectives and altering your perception of situations and challenges. Self-help writers have offered variations on this theme; Napoleon Hill referred to it as his board of directors and Jose Silva as his laboratory counsellors. Whatever, you decide to call your 'Team X', the technique of borrowing another's mindset can be a very powerful tool for solution finding. Overall it's best if your team are people to whom you do not have a strong emotional attachment. Try to think of mentors or experts in the field who will give you an objective expert opinion. It can be anyone from past, present or pure imagination. It can even be past and present versions of you.

- Visit your confidence lab and if you don't already have one, create a large conference table (or the kitchen table).
- Sit at the table and visualize the confidence dilemma as you prepare for the arrival of your crew.
- Imagine there is a knock at the door. Go over to the door, pause, and open it to welcome your first crew member. (Be prepared for anyone to be there. It may be one of the people you have already imagined or it might be someone who 'takes you by surprise'.)
- Greet them and invite them to sit at the table.
- Repeat for as many knocks on the door as come. The numbers may vary each time. It just might be one or two people. Sometimes a committee may arrive.
- Once everyone is seated invite them to introduce themselves.
- Next tell them your dilemma or challenge and go to each one in turn and ask them for their impressions.
- When they have all offered something, ask each of your crew if they have anything to add.

- Thank your crew (advisors) one by one as you see them out of your confidence lab.
- Take a moment to pause alone in your lab, knowing that ideas, solutions, ways forward are beginning to form.
- Count yourself back from 1 to 10, knowing that when you count 10 you will be alert and a solution will follow soon.
- Make notes of any immediate thoughts and impressions.
- Repeat the exercise as you feel necessary or if you want to gain further insight.

Although on first impressions this technique may seem a little bizarre, it is simply a way of altering your perceptual filters by thinking yourself into different perspectives. Once a solution emerges for your dilemma you can press forward and create an action plan to reach the goal which we'll cover in depth in the next chapter.

The next technique helps address the 'problem' of not being 'in the mood' and helps us to get there, at will. We may argue that we're not in the mood or not in the right frame of mind to tackle problems (find solutions). Or maybe we feel as if we've reached a dead end. Once in this mindset it may be difficult to break free from it. The strategic use of your imagination can help create a shift in these dead-end mindsets.

Changing States

Breathing and visualization techniques offer a quick and effective way to switch between emotional states. Simply by closing your eyes and taking a deep breath, your state changes. We discussed in Chapter 3 how the brain doesn't necessarily distinguish between reality and imagination. It also acts to create congruence between mind and body. This means that you can evoke a new state purely from your imagination. You don't have to wait passively to get into the right mood, you can actively take yourself there. Here's a simple technique to help you alter your mindset when you choose. We'll use the example of quiet confidence.

Preparation

- Use the information from your analysis of skills, strengths and situations where you experience higher confidence, or moments when you are most yourself and comfortable in your own skin, such as relaxing doing a hobby.
- Pick a trigger word that you want to link with the state. For instance, when I'm facing a challenge, I use the phrase 'Let's go.' However, you can simply name the state you want to evoke, so you could just say 'confident' or 'in the zone'. Whatever works for you. It's just something that acts as a cue for the process.

The Technique

- Breathe and relax.
- Imagine a time when you experienced quiet confidence.
- Recall as much of the detail as you can. What were the sights, sounds and other sensations? How were you feeling at the time? Summon these emotions. Attempt to re-experience the bodily sensations too, including the body language.
- Now consider on a scale of 0–10 how real it is: 0 equals not at all, and 10 equals 'It's as if I was really there.' Consider what would take you a step higher.
- If it's a 5, what does it need to get you to a 6, then a 7? Keep adding more detail from all of your senses. Make the image or experience brighter or less bright, or make the sounds louder or quieter. Use your preferred senses. Use whatever makes it more real for you.
- What will it take to get it to an 8, 9 or even 10? Keep adding the detail and acting into the experience so that it's as 'real' and 'alive' as you can make it, until it's good enough.

- Now add your trigger word or phrase (such as, 'confidence')
  to enhance it. Breathe deeply and repeat it a few times,
  feeling the sense of quiet confidence deepening.

You can adapt this technique for any state in which you'd like start the day or to give yourself an energy boost throughout the day. With practice, summoning different emotional states at will should become easier.

In the next section we consider a technique that brings together all of the principles learned so far.

Getting Over 'It'

Often, distressing or embarrassing events may return to haunt us, becoming increasingly more vivid every time we relive them and gaining more detail each time we recount the tale. Think about an experience that dented your confidence. Does reliving it in all its detail really help you to move on from it? Instead it may have become a compelling reason never to try again. Our inner critic often re-runs these old home movies. To make an image more compelling, we make it brighter, more vivid, bring it closer in our mind's eye and turn the volume up. Each time it becomes more real. So what if we reversed the process? What if we took away some of the vividness and clarity to lessen the emotional impact? Here's how:

Rewriting Bad Experiences

Experiment with this technique by choosing a mildly negative memory, something that dented your confidence but nothing too traumatic. A suggestion for this could be getting 'knocked back' when asking someone out for a coffee. With this in mind, read these instructions a few times so that you don't have to keep glancing at the book. It's important just to get the idea rather than follow the instructions to the letter.

- Breathe and relax.
- Focus on your negative memory and recall enough detail to return you to the experience.
- On a scale from 0 to 10 rate the intensity of the negative emotions associated with this memory: 0 means 'mild', 10 means 'the most incredibly painful memory you have', and 5 or 6 means 'moderately painful'.
- Notice how you are framing the image. Is the image up close? If so, does it become less intense if you take it further away? What's the rating now? Has the intensity reduced?
- Try projecting the image on to a movie screen so you are watching it, not living it. Rate the intensity now.
- Keep playing the movie and sit a few rows back in the cinema. How is that now?
- How does it feel as you move back a few more rows?
- Keep going until you are at the back of the cinema. Check the intensity again.
- Keep running your mental movie and have someone with very 'big hair' in your line of vision partially obscuring your view. How does it feel now?
- The audience gets pretty rowdy, rustling snack packets and slurping their drinks, and mobile phones keep going off. Add anything else you can think of to spoil the movie. The more ludicrous the better. Children screaming, farmyard animals or a clown with a fall-apart car.
- Keep running the movie and make it a pirate copy, with the obligatory person walking across the bottom of the screen, then coming back with a huge bucket of popcorn.
- Now you're in the projector room and viewing the movie through a little window.
- Change the movie into a small blurred black-and-white image with muffled sound. What's your emotional rating now?

- Now make it silent and add a totally inappropriate sound-track.
- Finally, run the film backwards until you're right back at the start. Rate the emotional intensity of this now.

The idea is that you've introduced elements to interrupt the compelling qualities of the original event. Have fun and do this a few times. You may also want to follow this up with the movie as you would have liked to have seen it, or just run the movie of the future desired outcome. You can also add a victorious soundtrack.

It is not necessarily appropriate to treat all memories this way. Some may be deeply significant moments, such as the loss of a loved one or the break-up of a relationship. The intention is not to trivialize these, so you may just want to do as much as needed to take the edge off the whole thing. So, for instance, you might move the image further away or change the scene into black and white. Even this small shift may help. Make the changes appropriate to the memory.

The Calmer–Confidence–Compassion Visualization

In psychology we know that the states of anxiety and relaxation cannot co-exist. In the *Dhammapada,* a collection of Buddhist maxims, there's one that says, 'Hatred cannot coexist with loving-kindness, and dissipates if supplanted with thoughts based on loving-kindness.' This saying inspired a technique used in the broaden-and-build approach (*Chapter 3*) called the loving-kindness meditation. I've adapted this technique to fit in with our goals of passing on confidence.

You Plus Three Technique

Preparation:

- Begin with long, slow deep breaths to relax.
- As you breathe out, repeat the word 'calmer' for a few breaths.
- Start by directing feelings of calm, confidence and compassion to yourself.
- Smile and mentally repeat the words 'calm, confidence and compassion' for a few breaths.
- Then reflect on your positive qualities, and make a positive statement about yourself.
- Continue to direct feelings of calm, confidence and compassion to yourself.
- Now direct your attention to someone (not a family member or friend), whom you admire and respect; it could be a respected public figure or a spiritual leader.
- Direct feelings of calm, confidence and compassion to them and see them smiling at you (and sending feelings of calm, confidence and compassion).
- Take a moment to experience the positive feelings.
- Now imagine a close friend, a family member or a loved one and direct feelings of calm, confidence and compassion to them.
- See them smiling and redirecting the feelings back to you, taking a moment to experience the feelings.
- Now imagine a neutral person about whom you have no special feelings, such as a shopkeeper or the person who delivers the post.
- Direct feelings of calm, confidence and compassion to them and see them smiling at you (and sending feelings of calm, confidence and compassion back).

- Take a moment to experience the positive feelings.
- Now consider a 'difficult person' in your life, someone you are currently having issues with.
- Direct feelings of calm, confidence and compassion to them and see them smiling at you (and sending feelings of calm, confidence and compassion back).
- Take a moment to experience these feelings.
- Now bring your attention back to you and direct the feelings of calm, confidence and compassion to yourself.
- Smile and repeat the mantra.
- After taking a few long, slow, deep breaths, open your eyes and return your awareness to your surroundings. Alternatively you can continue to stage two.

Stage Two – Directional Diffusion Technique

This follows on from the You Plus Three Technique or you can use it on its own. After a few long slow deep breaths, begin by directing the feelings of calm, confidence and compassion to yourself. Next direct the feelings to all points of the compass (north, south, east and west). Do this one direction at a time. Imagine the feelings coming back to you on each occasion. Next direct the feelings upwards and downwards and each time imagine the feelings coming back to you. Now imagine the feelings radiating from you and being sent all around. Experience the feelings of calm, confidence and compassion coming back to you.

Stage Three: Taking It Out

The calmer–confidence–compassion visualization does not have to be confined to indoor practice. You can take it out and about with you and make it part of your everyday interactions. Sitting on the bus or in traffic jams is a good time to practise it. Whether, sitting in a café, walking in the park, going to the supermarket, at work, the people and places to which you can direct these positive feelings are endless. Even if you're not religious you can visit cathedrals and churches and light a candle and let calmness–confidence–compassion radiate.

The calmer–confidence–compassion visualization is a great technique to form the basis of fulfilling the *Confidence-Karma* mandate of passing on confidence. Practised regularly, it will open up opportunities to take small, significant actions to boost and build confidence in others.

Positive-Outcome Prophecy

Although it explores the realms of imagination this chapter is still all about action rather than just reflection. These techniques require immersion. You have to do the exercises to judge their efficacy. Rubbing your chin sagely and saying 'Mmm that sounds interesting,' is not enough. Self-fulfilling prophecies don't have to be negative predictions. Confidence building is all about imagination, hopefulness, faith and well-directed action. The tactical use of our imagination becomes a driving force in helping us to take ownership, re-tune our filters, focus on solutions and create positive-outcome prophecies, that come true.

Something Else for the One-Minute Promo

Thoughts, feelings, attitudes and values:

Review: Finding Your Keys

Review the *Confidence-Karma Chain* to see how the things we have considered in this chapter relate to other aspects of confidence building. We have worked on a number of links in the chain: feelings, actions and thoughts; environmental situations and people; values and attitudes; skills and strengths. Take time to consider the review questions and note the answers in your journal.

- How do you rate your confidence at the end of this chapter?
- What's better for you in terms of confidence?
- What have been the most effective aspects of this chapter in taking you forward?
- What knock-on effects do you imagine there will be when you put the information in this chapter into practice?

Karma Call

How do these new insights help you to build confidence in others. Write down three affirmative actions you will take to continue the process. What will you pass on to other people in your life? 'In order to see changes, what changes will you be?'

1.

2.

3.

In the next chapter, we explore raising aspirations and aiming higher with goal setting.

Chapter 9

Raising Aspirations, Part 2: Future Desired Outcomes

One's reach should exceed one's grasp,
Or what's a heaven for?

Robert Browning, 1812–1889, poet and playwright

Preview

This chapter continues the process of raising aspirations by considering goals and the benefit of linking them with values and strengths.

Regret-Proof Your Life

It's often said that at their life's end people regret the things they haven't done rather than the things that they did. A nurse named Bronnie Ware talked to dying patients and recorded their top five regrets. The results were surprisingly unsensational. Her findings provide a recipe within the reach of everyone. Here's what she found:

- I wish I'd had the courage to live a life true to myself, not the life others expected of me.
- I wish I hadn't worked so hard.
- I wish I'd had the courage to express my feelings.
- I wish I had stayed in touch with my friends.
- I wish that I had let myself be happier.

What will you do, today, to build happiness and regret-proof your life?

Throughout *Unlock Your Confidence* you have been invited to set small goals and take action on them. These have included being true to yourself (*Chapter 5 on values*), life-work balance and just having fun (*Chapter 3*). The courage to express your feelings is a running theme throughout the book, as is the importance of relationships to other people. Happiness was also covered in Chapter 3 and we continue that theme in this chapter with goal setting. Goal setting is another key skill for building resilience and growing confidence. To build anything we begin with a plan. Goal setting is all about creating compelling action plans. This is in contrast to the idea many people have of goal setting, which is coloured by their experience of making New Year resolutions. These tend to fizzle out after a few weeks leaving a sense of failure. If goals are poorly planned they can dent your confidence. Goals are more likely to succeed if they tap into your sense of purpose, play to your strengths and meet your values. This chapter looks at a number of techniques to create compelling action plans for your future desired outcomes. We begin by considering different types of goals.

Different Types of Goals

Goals can be anything from magnificent life-changing, character-building, soul-defining aspirations to those all-too-often over-looked, simple daily uplifts, and anything else in between. We can set goals in just about any area of our lives. There are basically three types of goals:

- What we want to do (**doing**).
- What we want to have or get (**getting**).
- What we want to be (**being**).

Doing Goals

Doing goals are performance goals, they are action-oriented. These goals add to our sense of achievement, our skills and our strengths.

Doing goals are important for confidence building, since people often speculate about what they would do if they had more confidence. However, creating a compelling action plan and then taking action can build confidence. Doing goals can involve sporting activities, hobbies, doing household tasks, or work-based activities.

What are your doing goals?

Getting Goals

Getting goals (having goals) are about things that we would like to have. These can include having a family, getting a successful career, a loving relationship, a good sex life and so on. However, they often have an emphasis on material gains such as getting a new car, a bigger house and designer clothes. It's sometimes easier to get something that makes us feel good rather than work directly on thoughts and feelings. Getting new clothes can help us to feel confident but this means that the confidence remains dependent on material objects. There's nothing wrong with getting goals as long as they don't become a substitute for personal growth.

What are your getting goals?

Being Goals

Being goals focus on personal aspirations, that is how we would like to be ideally, such as to be a better communicator, to be confident, to be a better listener, and so on. These goals are somewhat difficult to quantify. What exactly does better mean? It is important to be able to translate these goals into actions, that is into a number of doing goals. What concrete actions constitute 'being confident'? The 0–10 scale (and accompanying questions) are particularly useful to help measure before and after effects of taking action.

What are your being goals?

Doing, being and getting goals can be about acquiring something new, but they can also be about maintaining something we already have, in particular our skills and strengths.

Maintenance Goals

Maintenance goals are about recognizing that skill acquisition is an on-going process. Athletes and musicians keep doing what they are good at, so they stay good. It's the same with any of your skills and strengths. You got good at something or discovered you had an aptitude for it. This was also shaped by your attitudes. Liking something and being good at something often go hand in hand. We are also likely to spend more time doing things we like and things we are good at. Setting maintenance goals is about developing strengths and skills. If there is any resistance to the goal-setting process, maintenance goals are a good place to start. You become familiar with the process at the same time as doing something you enjoy and maintaining an existing strength (or skill) So consider these questions:

- Thinking about your skills and strengths, how did you get good at those things? What did you do?
- What might you do to continue to sharpen and refine your skills and strengths?
- What opportunities are there to practise those skills and strengths?
- What opportunities are there to stretch those skills?

What are your maintenance goals?

Working through the goal-setting process with skills and strengths will help to build confidence in the process. You will then be able to transfer your success strategy to other goals.

Being In Flow

Being 'in flow' is that state of being completely and utterly absorbed in something. It's about having experiences when we lose all sense of time, such as doing a hobby or reading a good book. The concept was first described by Positive Psychologist Mihaly Csikszentmilhalyi (pronounced 'chick-SENT-me-high'!) in his classic work *Flow*. He explains how happiness is not something we leave to chance. For Csikszentmilhalyi, happiness is being in flow. We do this by setting goals that totally absorb us and stretch our abilities. The more time we spend in flow, the happier we are. Many people experience flow when they play computer games when hours pass by unnoticed. The key element with a computer game is the pursuit of skill and mastery. Think about any skill that you voluntarily tried to master and the hours you put in to achieve it. Suddenly you 'get it' and everything falls into place. How do you feel at that moment? You hit a peak because you pursued a peak experience. It's something we are motivated to do as children, whether it's walking a few extra steps or surpassing our personal best. As Robert Browning says 'our reach should exceed our grasp'. Being in flow is about investing ourselves in realistic but demanding goals in line with our values and strengths. Setting goals that put us into flow also builds confidence.

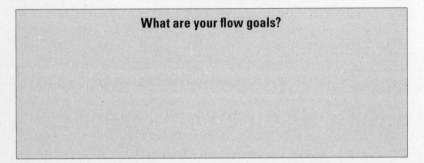

What are your flow goals?

Having set the scene for goal setting, the following sections will help you in selecting a longer-term goal and subject it to analysis with a number of tools and techniques in order to create a compelling action plan. We begin with a life-balance analysis to help you to decide in which area of your life you'd like to set a goal.

Life-Balance Analysis

Staff development departments run courses on 'work–life balance'. However, it's hardly a balance if on one side we have 'work' and on the other side every other aspect of our lives. 'Life' is a pretty broad category so we need to unpack exactly what it means. The work–life balance also begins with 'work', suggesting that life is just there to balance out the stresses of work. It's a hefty value judgement and doesn't really take into account any sense of growth. It seems to suggest simply juggling things about to maintain the status quo. I argue that we need to broaden out the scope of this black-and-white view of our lives and add in the value of growth (personal development). And here's another triangle to do just that.

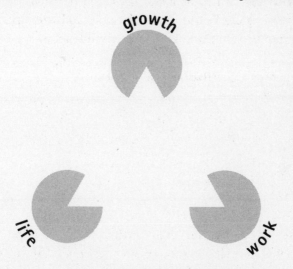

The Life–Work–Growth Triangle

Considering the interactions between these three points gives us a whole new take on things. Ponder the relationships. It's no longer about life playing a supporting, balancing role to work. Anyone who's ever experienced ill health or disturbed sleep will know how this can have a knock-on effect in all aspects of life. The same is true of positive experiences. Attention to relaxation opportunities has a positive effect on all aspects of our lives.

To consider the full definition of life (of which work is a part), the following life-balance analysis exercise offers ten life areas to rate using the 0–10 scale for satisfaction. Sometimes some areas of our lives get more attention than others by necessity. Feel free to replace any of these areas with ones of your own. My suggestions are:

- Health & well-being – any aspect of physical and psychological health.
- Wealth and finances.
- Home and environment.
- Fun (use of leisure time, hobbies, interests, laughter and so on).
- Relaxation.
- Support network (friends and family).
- Intimacy.
- Vocation (job, career, calling, professional life).
- Personal growth (opportunities for learning and growth).
- Spirituality (however you define it; alternatively replace it with something more appropriate for you).

On a scale from 0 to 10, rate your satisfaction for each of these life areas, where 0 means 'not at all satisfied' and 10 equals 'totally satisfied'. Circle whichever number reflects your satisfaction right now. For each of the life areas put a tick next to the number that represents 'good enough'.

Health	Wealth	Home	Fun	Relaxation	Support	Intimacy	Vocation	Growth	Spirituality
10	10	10	10	10	10	10	10	10	10
9	9	9	9	9	9	9	9	9	9
8	8	8	8	8	8	8	8	8	8
7	7	7	7	7	7	7	7	7	7
6	6	6	6	6	6	6	6	6	6
5	5	5	5	5	5	5	5	5	5
4	4	4	4	4	4	4	4	4	4
3	3	3	3	3	3	3	3	3	3
2	2	2	2	2	2	2	2	2	2
1	1	1	1	1	1	1	1	1	1
0	0	0	0	0	0	0	0	0	0

Choose one of these life areas to work with. I suggest you focus on an area that you feel is also most likely to increase your confidence too. Now consider these questions:

- What is it that tells you that you are at this point and not at 0?
- What is it that has helped you get from 0 to where you are now?
- How did you do this?
- If it's 0, what are you doing to keep it there?
- What are you doing, that you could do a bit more of, to increase your satisfaction?
- What do you imagine will be happening for you, when you move one point up the scale?
- What represents 'good enough' for you and how will you know you are there?

- What actions might you take to get from where you are now to 'good enough'?

It may help first to work on a simple goal to familiarize yourself with the various goal-setting models. Review your statements from Chapter 1 describing what confidence means to you. Then repeat the process with a longer-term goal of say six to twelve months.

Goal:

The wording doesn't have to be perfect at this stage, we work on that next, with the SMARTER technique.

Being SMARTER About Goals

Goals need to be well-formed. To achieve this we can use the simple SMARTER formula. Let's consider each stage with an example from your personal definition of confidence from Chapter 1. Select one statement from your list in Chapter 1 describing what confidence means to you. I'll offer a few examples here. A short-term goal might be to improve communication skills and a longer-term goal could be to get back into education.

- **Specific** – Goals should be about particular behaviours rather than general intentions. 'Being more confident' is rather vague and all-encompassing; 'being able to talk to strangers' is more specific. It has begun to focus the goal and make it more concrete. Now ask what, why, where, when, how and who questions. These help identify exactly what you want to accomplish, the benefits of accomplishing the goal, where you are going to do it, and who else is involved. It may not involve all strangers, at all times, everywhere you encounter them. It might be as simple as striking up a conversation in a coffee shop. For the education goal, decide what subject you want to study, at what level and where, and so on.

- **Measurable** – It's important that you can check objectively that the goal is on track and when it has been reached. Making goals behaviour-based helps to make them measurable. Asking 'how' questions helps. How much? How many? How often? How will I know when I've achieved it? It also helps to create a step-by-step plan for milestones (sub-goals) so that you can keep track of progress. This also helps to maintain motivation. Remember that the milestones need to stretch you (a little) too. So you might want to set yourself the task of striking up a conversation with two strangers in a coffee shop on five separate occasions (a total of ten conversations). You can tick them off as you achieve them. If you're returning to education, you'll know you're progressing as you attend classes and do assignments. There'll be a fixed number of assignments and you'll get grades to review your progress.

- **Achievable** – It's important to check if your goal is attainable. How will it be achieved? To build confidence, goals need to stretch us but still be within reach. If it's too difficult, even impossible, it will dent our confidence when we struggle to achieve it, and if too easy we will become bored. Ask, how can I accomplish this goal? It helps to know and review our strengths and limitations. For some people the 'coffee shop' goal might seem too easy. However, if you haven't been out of the house and spoken to a stranger in five years then it may seem very daunting. We often see the importance of achievability around health-based goals, where people commit to 'too much too soon' and you'd have to be superhuman to complete it. I'm thinking of the glut of 'New Year, New You' plans people commit to. For the education goal you wouldn't consider doing a PhD if you've been out of the education system for years. Instead, your goal would reflect the next logical step from where you are now.

- **Realistic and relevant** – If the goal is relevant the goal will drive you forward. Does it support other goals? Is it worthwhile to you? Does it match your skills, strengths, values and needs? Is this a good time? Are other factors supporting the goal or creating obstacles? Can you make five separate trips to a coffee shop and is there one close by? If you live in the middle of nowhere and have to make a three-hour round-trip to the nearest town, it's hardly realistic. So you should look for opportunities closer to home. We see the importance of being realistic when people start a diet the week before Christmas. The whole daredevil approach to confidence building lacks relevance for many people. Will leaping off a tall building really give you the confidence to ask someone out on a date? Probably not, but practising talking to strangers in coffee shops may well do. It may not be as exciting and sexy but it's far more relevant. For the education goal, you wouldn't take on a massive workload without thinking about existing commitments and what support you would need. So you might consider on-line or distance learning where you can study at your own pace. Similarly you wouldn't study geography if your ultimate goal was to be a surgeon.

- **Time-bound** – This means having a time scale and target date. If you don't set a time frame then there is no sense of urgency to the goal. End states need end dates. A commitment to a deadline helps to focus your efforts, otherwise your goals can become sidelined by the demands of everyday life. The key question is: by what date will it be achieved? It's also helpful to have dates for when milestones (sub-goals) will be achieved. A goal without a target day is really just a dream. Will it really achieve anything if those five trips to the coffee shop are spread out over 15 years? However, if you set the target date for two weeks ahead then it creates more of a sense of urgency. It also means that you are more likely to build on the experience each time. Education goals usually have built-in time limits.
- **Enthusiastic and positively worded** – It's important for your goal to describe the end state you are moving towards. Focus on attainment not loss. This uses the same principle as writing positive affirmations in the previous chapter. Notice we didn't say 'I want to be able walk into a coffee shop and not ignore strangers and not ignore opportunities to chat.' Once you've worked out what you don't want then rephrase the goal in terms of what you do want; emphasize the behaviour you want to move towards.
- **Regularly reviewed** – As not all factors are known when you initially set a goal, it's good to review your progress to ensure you are still on track and, if not, make adjustments so that you keep moving forward. Stumbles and delays are just that; they are not failure. Use the feedback and adjust. You may realize that two chats every coffee-shop visit are too much. You may find that some times are better than others to initiate conversations. So be prepared to adjust your goal slightly, as long as it still feels like an accomplishment. The

classic problem with New Year resolutions is that people don't review and adjust but give up instead.

Setting a Target Date

For longer-term goals it is sometimes not so easy to predict an end date as it is for short-term goals. Here are two ways to help you set realistic target dates:

- Count forward based on your realistic milestones (from your SMARTER analysis) to establish the final date for the goal.
- Count backwards from a predicted date (using the milestones) to the present date. This will help verify whether the goal is achievable and realistic. If not, adjust the predicted date.

Write down your reworded SMARTER goal that will take you from where you are now on your life-satisfaction scale to where you would like to be.

SMARTER goal:

Next perform a SWOT analysis on your SMARTER goal. Consider **strengths, weaknesses, opportunities** and **threats.**

For the coffee-shop goal, strengths might include general conversation skills with familiar people. A weakness might be a tendency to clam up in front of strangers, so that's where regular practice with the relaxation techniques is useful. Remember, though, that not saying much in front of strangers is not necessarily a bad thing. Use the material from Chapter 4 to perfect your listening skills. Many people like a good listener. You may realize that it doesn't have to be the coffee shop. Consider other places where you might strike up conversations. 'Threats' sound a bit ominous. It's not necessarily so. It's pretty similar to checking how achievable and realistic something is. For instance if you have a really important work deadline then you may not be able to keep nipping out for coffee.

There is an element of repetition between SMARTER and SWOT and you may find that you prefer one to the other. The important thing is that you create a really detailed action plan, not which technique you favour. You may find that with SMARTER and SWOT you have already created a really compelling action plan. However, if you still feel you need a final layer of detail, then you can apply the goal-setting technique GO-FLOW.

GO-FLOW

GO-FLOW is my adaptation of the **GROW** (Goals, Reality, Options, Will) model, originally used in psychotherapy. It was adapted and popularized by John Whitmore. GO-FLOW serves to remind us that goals can help create a state of flow as opposed to just 'going with the flow'. It stands for:

- **Goal** – analysed and stated using the SMARTER criteria.
- **Observation** – observing opportunities, reality and choices. This may offer you ideas of how to achieve your goal in slightly different ways. For the education goal this might be about doing some research to find out what courses are out there, including locations and timetables. This includes a realistic appraisal of your circumstances. When interviewing

prospective candidates for my psychology course I asked the question 'What will you give up in life to make way for this course?' Many have told me that it was one of the most important questions they had ever been asked.

- **Feelings** – checking you are aligning your feelings, perceptions, emotions and attitudes to the goal. At this stage if you have feelings of trepidation then go back to SWOT and focus on your strengths.
- **Limitations or Let-Downs** – considering the limitations (obstacles and barriers) for this goal, how you can counter them and how you will deal with let-downs (you can also use SWOT to help you here). By attempting to predict obstacles, we are less likely to be overwhelmed when they occur.
- **Options** – considering all possible ways of achieving the same outcome. This is where an assessment of values helps (*Chapter 5*). Remember the potential MBA student who ended setting up his own business instead? For education, there are a range of options – full-time courses, part-time courses, distance learning, etc.
- **Will** – I will do it.

Taken together these tools can help create compelling action plans. Whereas SMARTER focuses on goal definition, GO-FLOW emphasizes the importance of planning the process. It also expressly focuses on feelings which the other techniques do not. Sometimes, it is our feelings that are most likely to hold us back. Feelings of discomfort are easily translated into subjective feelings of incompetence. The beauty of all of these techniques is that they offer an objective view of circumstances and invite us to consider a much broader picture than we might have when 'locked in survival mode'. Feel free to mix and match SMARTER, SWOT and GO-FLOW.

It's helpful to run through the process with a small goal so that it's more familiar when tackling larger ones. The coffee-shop goal might be something you do as preparation for a plan to attend a networking meeting or go island-hopping in Greece on your own. For longer-term goals, the process is exactly the same.

What you have now is a detailed analysis of your goal. Next we consider other information to support your goal.

Supporting Your Goals

Motivation

It is vitally important to have a strong sense of ownership of your goals. You need to perceive them as worthwhile, that is, in support of your values, if you are to pursue them actively and effectively. Goals need to be rewarding (**positive reinforcement**) or help us move away from unpleasant consequences (**negative reinforcement**). Personally owned goals have a stronger intrinsic pull than those imposed on us (such as some work-related goals).

Our motivations are the fuel that keeps us moving towards our goals, especially when the initial excitement of goal setting evaporates (as can be the case with New Year resolutions). Our values and strengths are like renewable energy sources, our **internal motivators**, and internal positive reinforcement. They provide built-in rewards. By contrast, **external motivators**, often material rewards, still provide reinforcement but are fleeting or not a constant or reliable source. So, for instance, we can gain self-esteem by setting goals in line with our values that stretch us. Alternatively, we can buy a designer jacket, which will also boost our confidence or esteem for a while. However, as the jacket fades and wears out so does the self-esteem. Also, if we are only motivated by external sources, what happens when the money runs out? Do we also cease to reach for our goals? It's possible to use both type of motivator, but it's important to be aware of the differences, especially for longer-term goals.

This simple exercise will help to clarify your motivations. Think of a goal you would like to achieve and this time make it a slightly longer-term goal, say between one and three months. Using the following table, in the first column come up with three positive benefits of achieving this goal. In the second column think of three disadvantages (negative consequences) of NOT achieving it. If you can think of any more reasons, add those too.

My goal	
Positive benefits of achieving goal	Negative consequences of NOT achieving goal
1.	1.
2.	2.
3.	3.

This list gives you a double motivation: what the goal takes you towards and what it moves you away from. It is a good idea to review your list of motivators regularly, adding to it if you wish, to maintain your overall motivation. Wherever possible relate these motivations to your values. So let's consider your commitment to this goal.

Commitment

Rate your commitment to this goal on a scale from 0 to 10, where 0 equals 'no commitment at all' and 10 equals 'total commitment'.

0	1	2	3	4	5	6	7	8	9	10
None					Moderate					Total

- What is it that tells you that you are at this point and not at 0?
- What is it that has helped you get from 0 to where you are now?
- How did you do this?
- What are you doing, that you could do a bit more of, to increase your commitment?
- What do you imagine will be happening for you, when you move one point up the scale?
- What represents 'good enough' for you and how will you know you are there?
- What actions might you take to get from where you are now to 'good enough'?

If your commitment level doesn't match your 'good enough' figure, review your motivations in the exercise above. Add motivations until you reach your 'good enough' score.

Overcoming Obstacles

Considering your possible obstacles and limitations beforehand may make the difference between giving up and pushing on. Inevitably something may happen unexpectedly and we may have to deal with that when it comes. We are in a better position to do this if we have already taken stock of the expected. That way we can deal with problems quickly and get back on track.

Take a sheet of paper and draw a line down the middle. On the left hand-side make a list of possible obstacles. On the right hand-side list the obstacle removers and neutralizers in the form of your strengths, skills, and the techniques in this book, as well as other resources you could use and people you could call on for help.

Obstacles to goal achievement	Strengths, resources, strategies
1.	1.
2.	2.
3.	3.

Having made this list, you are less likely to get thrown off course. There may be slight delays but this means you just adjust the target date and sub-goals and get back on track.

Sub-Goals as Milestones

Sub-goals act as milestones or signposts to overall goal progress. These smaller steps need to have an element that stretches us so that we are able continually to build on a sense of achievement and so build confidence and motivation.

Break your overall goal down into a series of steps or smaller goals. For the purposes of this exercise the following exercise suggests six sub-goals. However, in reality every goal is different. Set as many sub-goals as it takes. Each has its own target date.

		Milestones (Sub-goals)			
1	2	3	4	5	6
When?	When?	When?	When?	When?	When?

Creating sub-goals also helps you to predict, more accurately, the final target date. So at this point, double check your original estimate to make sure it is realistic and achievable. If at any time you find you are not running to schedule, then take remedial action and if necessary adjust the target dates for your sub-goals. If you get stuck at one place, ask yourself whether there is anything else you could be getting on with. Adjust the target date if necessary.

Here's a visualization technique to support goal setting.

Getting to GRIPs with Goals

The GRIP technique has four stages:

- **Goal** – set a clear, well-defined goal.
- **Relax** – induce your relaxation response.
- **Image** – imagine and visualize an image, bring all of your senses into play.
- **Persistence** – focus on it often.

Goal

The first stage is to set your goal, using the processes from this chapter – SMARTER, SWOT and GO-FLOW – to produce your well-formed outcome.

Relax
The second stage is to use a relaxation technique (*see Chapter 3*) to induce your relaxation response with any method you desire. If you want to deepen your relaxation then add one of the visualizations such as your ideal place (sanctuary) before proceeding to the third stage.

Image
In this stage, we create a mental image of the outcome by visualizing the finishing line, that is, the completed goal – your preferred positive outcome. Use your senses to add detail to create a vivid, compelling picture of achievement (*see Chapter 8*).

Persistence
Persistently tuning into images of your future desired outcome incorporates it in your perceptual filters. So take advantage of any breaks or quiet times of the day to combine imagery and visualization during your relaxation exercises and add a few energizing breaths too to create positive physical associations.

Finally, an important part of goal setting is to acknowledge your achievement.

Celebrate
Mark your sub-goals with small celebrations and the goal's full completion with a more significant act of celebration. Consider in advance what the rewards will be. This will add to your motivation too.

This method is very detailed and requires substantially more time investment than the ill-fated New Year resolution. However, the success rate for well-designed action plans is much higher than a vague idea thrown together at the end of December, labouring under the illusion that 1 January is the only time to set goals. Ultimately, the imperative of one special day is never a strong enough motivation to keep us going when we encounter obstacles or frustrations. Well-formed, well-prepared action plans prepare the way for success.

Mission Tweet

The social networking site Twitter is all about brevity. Users send and read text-based messages, known as tweets, of up to 140 characters. Working with this limit, how would you state your mission in life? What do you aim to achieve that will give your life meaning? To test out the character limit, I posted the following tweet (@drgarywood):

> 'What is your mission statement, that includes your strengths, values, goals, the people you will work with and the difference you will make?'

So how would you respond, in around 20 words? People often use abbreviations and 'text-speak' on Twitter to get around the limitation. However, your mission tweet should only contain complete words (not even an ampersand). Anyone reading your mission statement should be able to discern your values and strengths. It should contain a sense of an overall life goal and what action you will take to achieve it. So if I wanted to strip my mission right down to the bare bones I'd say:

> 'My mission in life is to empower people to develop.'

That's only 10 words and 51 characters but it's rather vague. It doesn't tell anyone how I intend to achieve this.

> 'My mission in life is to empower people to develop through coaching and evidence-based psychology.'

That's now 17 words and I still have 42 characters to spare. I could specialize and specify what types of people or add another skill but it's well on the way to communicating a guiding principle in my life. I could add 'and have fun doing it' and I've still got a few characters to spare. Essentially, using the *Confidence-Karma Approach* is like holding a mirror up to yourself and your life so that you get a better look at the positives. Your mission statement should reflect that. So now it's your turn. Consider these questions:

- What is my overall goal in life?
- Who do you want to work with to achieve this goal?
- What is that you wish to create with these people?
- What is it that you want to do to achieve your goal with other people?

My mission in life (in 140 characters or less) is . . .

#ConfidenceKarma

Now that you have your mission statement, consider what contribution goals you will set. This includes the *Confidence-Karma* goal of passing confidence on to other people. If you wish add the hashtag at the end so that all of our tweets can be easily recognized.

Contribution Goals

Contribution goals are not necessarily about grand gestures Setting up a Twitter account and tweeting inspiration goals is a contribution (see @confidencekarma). It might be using your letter-writing skills to get the local council to improve the area where you live (for you and everyone else). It might be volunteering in a charity shop or contributing to hospital radio, starting up a neighbourhood watch scheme or visiting older neighbours for a chat. It could be shopping ethically and supporting companies who are environmentally friendly and don't use child slave labour. It might be committing to recycling or simply using the insights from this book to help build confidence in others. One-off acts of generosity are great, but imagine how things would change if we all committed regularly to contribution goals, no matter how tiny. Think of the difference it would make.

With this in mind, what will your on-going contributions be? The important thing is to select a goal that upholds your values, uses your strengths and demonstrates your mission statement. Review your notes from the chapter-end Karma Calls. What did you try? Of all the things you tried what had the most impact on the lives of others and what gave you a confidence boost? This shows the way for longer-term confidence goals. Building confidence is about having the courage to regret-proof your life and help other people to do the same.

Something Else for the One-Minute Promo

Thoughts, feelings, attitudes, strengths and values:

Review: Finding Your Keys

Review the *Confidence-Karma Chain* in Chapter 1 to see how the things we have considered in this chapter relate to other aspects of confidence building. It has focused on creating action plans for you to set personal development goals.

- How do you rate your confidence at the conclusion of this chapter on the scale of 0–10?
- What's better for you in terms of confidence?
- What have been the most effective aspects of this chapter in taking you forward?
- What knock-on effects do you imagine there will be when you put the information in this chapter into practice?

Karma Call

How do these new insights help you to build confidence in others. Write down three affirmative actions you will take to continue the process. What will you pass on to other people in your life? 'In order to see changes, what changes will you be?'

1.

2.

3.

In the next chapter, we consider an exercise to bring most aspects of *Confidence Karma* together to create guiding themes for future action.

Chapter 10

Selling Yourself ...
Not Selling Yourself Short

As is our confidence, so is our capacity.

William Hazlitt, 1778–1830, essayist, critic, philosopher

Preview

In the final chapter we review the themes from the book and draw together the information for that all important one-minute promo.

What Goes Around Comes Around

And so here we are at the final stage in exploring the principles of the *Confidence-Karma Approach*, but this is by no means the final stage in the journey. The aim of this chapter is to provide a focus for your confidence building and a method with which you can take things forward. This book provides the principles for confidence but it doesn't supply all the answers. That's your job. The answers are in the application. Even if you were to engage me as a coach, I wouldn't be following you around on a bike shouting to you through a megaphone. However, I hope that the questioning style I use in this book has got into your system and has become an integral part of how you view the world. Confidence is a process and now you know how to do it.

Your *Confidence-Karma* journey began by getting baseline information about where you were at that moment in time. Behind what many people call chance or luck is often a great deal of preparation. Roman Emperor Marcus Aurelius said, 'Look well into thyself; there is a source of strength which will always spring up if thou wilt always look there.' So, in the second stage of the journey, you focused on looking for what shines and sparkles (strengths and skills). You also considered patterns of fluctuation in your confidence, to spot the most favourable conditions. Again, preparation can create better chances.

Now, in case you hadn't noticed, the master key of confidence is relaxation. If you want to feel more comfortable in your own skin, just do it. What followed was an impression-management course, considering how the small stuff can make a big difference. If you followed the exercises you did a whole lot of small stuff. At the heart of the *Confidence-Karma Approach* are the concepts of attitudes and values. As psychologist William James said, 'Human beings, by changing the inner attitudes of their minds, can change the outer aspects of their lives.' Confidence is an attitude and so is 'lack of confidence'. If the lack isn't supporting life goals, then look for evidence to change the attitude. Create a state of readiness and take action. Confidence and self-esteem come easier when we remove the blockages, and drop defence mechanisms that only serve to distort our sense of self.

Three attitudes that help us look to the future are control, commitment and challenge. All three are woven throughout the *Confidence-Karma Approach*. They help to build resilience in the face of life changes. Finally, to build confidence and self-esteem we need to aim higher and raise our aspirations. And once you have done all that, the penultimate challenge of this book won't look nearly as daunting as it did before.

And so it all leads to this:

One-Minute Promo – The Final Draft

Now I'm aware that speaking in public is one of the things that strikes fear in the hearts and minds of people, second only to death. At this point you're probably asking 'Does anyone have any hot coals I can dance on?' So let's be clear. Speaking in public is not the task. The real task is to prepare a one-minute presentation from the information you have collected from the exercises in this book and just deliver it in front of a mirror, without an audience. No one else needs to see the presentation and no one even needs to see your preparation notes.

The One-Minute Promo brings together many of the themes of the book. That's why I summarized them above. It will help to consolidate all the information you've read and experienced through the exercises. It's not enough to 'get it', you have to 'do it' too. This exercise becomes your manifesto for moving forward in life. It represents a guiding light for how you present yourself to the world from now on. It's also a challenge to 'walk the talk', or as the quaint old expression has it, 'to put your money where your mouth is'. Part of passing on confidence is leading by example. You've put all the hard work in, so make it count.

The Research

Review the previous chapters and collect the notes you made in the One-Minute Promo boxes. It may help to copy them on to separate sheets of paper so that you can move them around and notice the themes and patterns. Review your mission statement from the previous chapter. You can use this for the opening statement:

1. Introduce yourself ('Hello, I'm <name>') and then paraphrase your mission statement. It establishes everything anyone needs to know about you and provides a structure for the rest of the promo.

Ideally your mission statement contains something about your goals (*Chapter 9*), your strengths (*Chapter 2*) and your values (*Chapter 5*). So you might want to create three separate sections. Begin with values, then move on to strengths and end with goals. Now consider the timings. Allow about 10 seconds for your opening statement. For values, strengths and goals allow 15 seconds each. This leaves 5 seconds for a short snappy closing phrase. Think about how you would sum up your values, strengths and goals in 15 seconds each (which is probably going to be about 30 words). Rather than make an abstract statement add a sense of how. Illustrate a value and strength by giving an example of actions you take to demonstrate these. For the overall goal also say how, and also bear in mind that the strengths and values are the justification for this goal.

- My values are:

- My strengths are:

- My main goal in life is:

Okay, those are my suggestions, but you may have other ideas that are equally valid or more so because you know yourself a lot better than I do.

Now let's review what skills you might need, plus I'll add a few more tips to the pot.

Skills

1. Breathing techniques and relaxation (stress-busting) (*Chapter 3*).
2. Impression management including body language (*Chapter 4*).
3. Getting in the right frame of mind (*Chapters 3 and 8*).
4. Mental rehearsal and visualizing a future desired outcome (*Chapter 8*).

It's just a matter of putting these together. As well as relaxation, practice is key. Reading from a piece of paper means you will keep glancing down at it and breaking eye contact. Memorize the information but don't just blurt it out word-for-word. If it means something to you, then you should be connecting with it emotionally. The script is there as a framework. Remember it's not Shakespeare so no one is going to tell you that you got it wrong. Gradually wean yourself off the paper by rehearsing in front of the mirror and then go for a 'take'.

When you are relatively satisfied would you be prepared to take it a step further?

Going Further

Tell a close friend what you have been doing and ask if you can give them your One-Minute Promo over a cup of coffee. Keep it informal and relaxed and get some feedback. Go back to the mirror and try it out again. How does it feel? Has it changed at all?

Next use your webcam or a video camera and record your One-Minute Promo. Don't censor or stop if you make a mistake. Just try it out a few times and review the recordings. Is there anything new you've noticed? Is it communicating what you want it to? Does it present you, truthfully, in the best possible light? If not, what will you change or enhance? And so on.

Now you could involve a group of friends in this project. Have a group coffee morning and take it in turns to give your presentations and give each other feedback. Take the next step and have everyone record their own piece and comment on each other's recordings. Finally, all get together and give your presentations to each other, live. Set ground rules beforehand, that it's supposed to be fun and uplifting and that all feedback should focus on building on the positives. If you need to give constructive feedback of what to improve, use the **sandwich technique**. That is, highlight something positive, then mention the area for improvement, then finish off with another positive.

Your One-Minute Promo is your declaration of intent to move forward into the future. So the question is, do you really believe it yet? Rate its believability on a scale from 0 to 10, where 0 equals 'totally unbelievable' and 10 equals 'totally believable'.

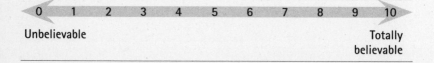

| 0 | 1 | 2 | 3 | 4 | 5 | 6 | 7 | 8 | 9 | 10 |

Unbelievable   Totally
                                                    believable

- What tells you that it's at this point on the scale and not one below or a 0?
- What do you imagine changing to move it one point along the scale (assuming it's not already a 10)?
- What score represents 'good enough' for you?

Review: Finding Your Keys

In this chapter you have revised most aspects of the *Confidence-Karma Approach*.

- How do you rate your confidence at the conclusion of this chapter?
- What's better for you in terms of confidence?
- What have been the most effective aspects of this chapter in taking you forward?
- What knock-on effects do you imagine there will be when you put the information in this chapter into practice?

Confidence Keys

Review the exercises and the entries in your journal and list your top ten confidence keys.

1.

2.

3.

4.

5.

6.

7.

8.

9.

10.

Confidence Rating

Think about the journey you made in this book and consider what impact it has had on your confidence rating, using the 0–10 scale, where 0 equals 'no confidence at all' and 10 equals 'total confidence'. You can use fractions of a point if you wish.

0	1	2	3	4	5	6	7	8	9	10
None					Moderate					Total

What are the important things you have discovered that will keep moving you forward to build and maintain your confidence?

Karma Call

Review all of your Karma Calls from the end of each of the chapters. Which actions could you work into longer-term goals? Alternatively what do you imagine doing on a daily basis to build confidence in others? What will you pass on to other people in your life? 'In order to see changes, what changes will you be?'

1.

2.

3.

And after this there's just a short story . . .

The Outro: All Souped Up

Little by little, a little becomes a lot.
Tanzanian Proverb

A man was amazed to see a sign at a local market offering 'magic soup stones' for sale. He had never heard of such a thing before and was partial to the odd gadget and bit of magic and so enquired. The market trader told him that it was the most miraculous of devices and made the most amazing soup by magic.

The man asked how it worked and the seller said, 'All you have to do is fill a pot with water and place the magic soup stone in the pot with a few other ingredients and it produces the most delicious soup.'

The man replied, 'That's amazing, what other ingredients will I need?' The trader responded, 'Just throw in a few things such as some chopped onions, a couple of sticks of celery, a few carrots, and the magic soup stone will do the rest.'

'Amazing,' exclaimed the man, 'and that's all I need to make the soup?' The trader replied, 'Well, just a few bay leaves, some rosemary and thyme and one or two sage leaves, and if you have some lean meat, that helps enhance the process.'

'That's incredible,' said the man, 'and how long does this take?' The trader told him, 'The magic is complete in just two hours, with stirring every half hour, and a pinch of salt and pepper.'

'I must have one,' said the man. 'How long does the magic work?' 'That's the miracle,' replied the trader. 'The magic soup stone will help you produce delicious, nutritious soup in this manner, whenever you want it, for the rest of your life.' The man bought the soup stone and used it as an ornament on his kitchen shelf with the number of his local takeaway etched into it.

I'd like to say that the last word goes to Samuel Johnson (1709–84), writer and lexicographer, who said,

'A writer only begins a book. A reader finishes it.'

However that honour goes to you. It's your life so take it personally. You have all the ingredients. This book has merely given you the key to unlock the store cupboard and given you the recipe. You now have the insights from the exercises and your journal. Most importantly, you have all the skills at your finger tips to go and make great soup. Make a lot of it, share it with others and help them to find their own recipes too!

Further Reading and Resources

As with any self-help book, the secret lies not in the reading but in taking action on the insights. Once you have worked through the exercises in the book, here are some resources to help you to explore the themes in the book in further detail. All links for websites were tested at the time of writing.

Next Step: Coaching (and Courses) with the Author

I provide one-to-one, solution-focused coaching for individuals and organizations and also run personal development courses in confidence building as well as mindfulness, meditation, creative visualization, motivation, goal setting and team building. The confidence course has a strong experiential emphasis. It follows the main principles of the book and includes exercises that benefit from interaction such as role play, improvization games and discussions. It's not an off-the-peg course but is led by the make-up of the group. For further details see:

> www.drgarywood.co.uk
> www.confidencekarma.org
> www.psycentral.wordpress.com

To discuss how coaching (and the courses) would benefit you or your organization, contact me by email: info@drgarywood.co.uk

Contact and Interaction with Gary Wood:

You are invited to follow, like and interact on the following social media platforms. I'm particularly interested in hearing your success stories and feedback from working with the book.

Twitter: @drgarywood.com and @confidencekarma
Facebook: drgarywoodpage
LinkedIn: drgarywood
Youtube: drgarywood

Three Inspirational Novels

Periodically, I re-read these three books in this order, and get something new from them every time.

Antoine de St-Exupéry, *The Little Prince* (Kathryn Woods translation), London: Picador Books, 1982
Richard Bach, *Jonathan Livingston Seagull: A Story*, London: HarperCollins, 1994
Richard Bach, *Illusions: The Adventures of A Reluctant Messiah*, London: Arrow Books, 2001

Here are suggestions to explore the various tools and techniques in greater detail:

Creative Visualization

Shakti Gawain, *Creative Visualization*, London: Bantam Books, 1982
Maxwell Maltz, *Psycho-Cybernetics*, London: Pocket Books, 1969

Goals

Mihaly Csikszentmihalyi, *Flow: The Classic Work on How to Achieve Happiness*, London: Rider, 2002
Gary Wood, *Don't Wait For Your Ship to Come In . . . Swim Out to Meet It: Tools and Techniques for Positive Lasting Change.* Chichester: Capstone, 2008

Meditation and Mindfulness

David Fontana, *Learn to Meditate*, London: Duncan Baird Publishers, 1999
Jon Kabat-Zinn, *Wherever You Go, There You Are: Mindfulness Meditation for Everyday Life*, London: Piatkus, 2004

Gender and Relationships

Gary W Wood, *Sex, Lies & Stereotypes: Challenging Views of Women, Men and Relationships*, London: New Holland, 2005

Contribution

Books
Anon., *Change the World for a Fiver: We Are What We Do*, London: Short Books, 2004
Michael Norton, *365 Ways to Change the World*, London: Harper-Perennial, 2006

Film
This feel-good film is all about making a contribution.

Pay It Forward (2000: Mimi Leder)

Websites
Here's a short list of contribution websites:

Amnesty International:	http://www.amnesty.org/
Fairtrade:	http://www.fairtrade.org.uk/
G.I.F.T	http://www.giveitforwardtoday.org/
Oxfam:	http://www.oxfam.org.uk/
Unicef:	http://www.unicef.org/
38 Degrees:	http://www.38degrees.org.uk/
Avaaz:	http://www.avaaz.org/

Self-Talk

Martin E P Seligman, *Learned Optimism: How to Change Your Mind and Your Life*, London: Free Press, 1998

Strengths

Books

Marcus Buckingham & Donald O Clifton, *Now, Discover Your Strengths*, London: Pocket Books, 2004

Martin Seligman, *Authentic Happiness*, London: Nicholas Brealey Publishing, 2003

Website

For Martin Seligman's *Authentic Happiness* homepage containing numerous on-line self-assessment questionnaires, go to:

http://www.authentichappiness.sas.upenn.edu/

Breathing

James E Loehr & J A Midgow, *Breath In, Breathe Out: Inhale energy and exhale stress by guiding and controlling your breathing.* Alexandria, Virginia: Time Life Books, 1986, 1989

Learning Websites

There are numerous free resources on the Web to allow you to explore your learning styles, including tips and strategies for becoming more flexible in your approach to learning. Some of them require you to sign up using an email address. I recommend that you set up an email address especially for your personal development. All links were live at the time of writing.

Index of Learning Styles (Soloman & Felder):
http://www.engr.ncsu.edu/learningstyles/ilsweb.html
Canfield's Learning Styles Inventory
http://www.tecweb.org/styles/canfield1.html
VARK Questionnaire
http://www.vark-learn.com/english/page.asp?p=questionnaire
Learning Styles Inventory
http://www.rrcc-online.com/~psych/LSInventory.html
Honey and Mumford's Learning Styles Questionnaire
http://www.peterhoney.com/